Praise for *Playing to Win*

"Reading *Playing to Win* is like having prime seats at the Super Bowl of strategy. You'll learn the strategies consumer goods powerhouse Procter & Gamble uses to get its innovative products into millions of homes—plus tested methods for winning your own marketplace contests. If you're a marketer or a leader, you need to read this book."

—Daniel H. Pink, author, *Drive* and *A Whole New Mind*

"This is the best book on strategy I have ever read. Lafley and Martin get to the heart of what's important: how to make choices in order to control events rather than allowing events to control your choices. Everyone wants to win; this book sets down with calm authority the steps you must take to turn aspiration into reality."

—Sir Terry Leahy, former CEO, Tesco

"Lafley and Martin teach us how to develop and then how to deploy strategy. Their recommendations apply at every level—corporation, business units, products, and teams. This is a great book."

—Clayton M. Christensen, Kim B. Clark Professor of
Business Administration, Harvard Business School;
author, *The Innovator's Dilemma*

"Most authors conduct research before they write a book. Lafley and Martin went out and did something. They used their simple, subtle framework—Where will we play? How will we win?—to double the value of one of the world's greatest businesses. And now they're showing you how to do the same. Read this book. . . before your competitors find it."

—Chip Heath, coauthor, *Decisive: How to Make Better Choices in Life and Work*

"*Playing to Win* is a rare combination of depth of thinking and ease of use. It clearly explains what business strategy is and isn't, and how to develop it. Lafley and Martin distill their hard-won experiences and offer insights, practical hands-on tools, and tips that will inspire and allow you to think strategically in new ways about your own business."

—Jørgen Vig Knudstorp, CEO, Lego Group

"A great CEO and a renowned educator join forces to create a must-read for anyone thinking about strategy."

—Jack Welch, former Chairman and CEO, General Electric

"Here is business strategy through the eyes of the man who led Procter & Gamble's stunning turnaround and success in the 2000s and the strategist who advised and worked with him. Lush with insights that show the 'what' and the 'how' of two master strategists."

—Scott Cook, cofounder and Chairman of the Executive Committee, Intuit

"Lafley and Martin have invested their respective careers in understanding the complexity of strategy. What has emerged in this seminal work is a simple and rich framework that can help business leaders think through strategic choices. It is an eminently helpful guide to choice making, which is the most essential part of leadership."

—James P. Hackett, President and CEO, Steelcase Inc.

"*Playing to Win* is an insightful do-it-yourself guide that demystifies what it takes to craft, implement, and continuously improve effective business strategies. Using relevant, real-world examples, Lafley and Martin offer proven techniques for competing and winning in today's challenging global business environment."

—Jim McNerney, President, CEO, and Chairman, Boeing

"I love this book; it is thought provoking and acts as a catalyst to ask questions—about ourselves and our business life course. In a day and age when information and instant communication are relentless components of business and our lifestyle, A.G. Lafley and Roger Martin suggest we take an important pause to actually question our strategic road maps and the associated plans we need in order to succeed in this marketplace."

—Thomas Tull, founder and CEO, Legendary Pictures

PLAYING TO WIN

PLAYING TO

WIN

HOW STRATEGY REALLY WORKS

A.G. LAFLEY
ROGER L. MARTIN

HARVARD BUSINESS REVIEW PRESS

Boston, Massachusetts

Library of Congress Cataloging-in-Publication Data

Lafley, A.G. (Alan G.)
  Playing to win : how strategy really works / A.G. Lafley and Roger L. Martin.
      p. cm.
  ISBN 978-1-4221-8739-5 (alk. paper)
  1. Strategic planning. 2. Success in business. 3. Organizational change. 4. Procter & Gamble Company. I. Martin, Roger L. II. Title.
  HD30. 28. L34 2013
  658.4'012—dc23

Inspired by Peter Drucker (1909–2005),
mentor and friend

Contents

How Strategy Really Works

This is a book about strategy, written by a former CEO and a business school dean. When we met, we were neither of those things. More than twenty years ago, when we first worked together on a study of P&G's distribution channels, it was as a category manager in P&G's laundry business and an outside consultant from a small but growing strategy firm called Monitor Company. Working on that assignment, we formed the basis of a very productive and very long friendship. By the time we became, respectively, CEO of P&G and dean of the Rotman School of Management, we were true thinking partners on strategy and worked together in earnest on the transformation of P&G between 2000 and 2009. This book is the story of that transformation and the approach to strategy that informed it. (Details on the results of the transformation may be found in appendix A.)

This approach grew out of the strategy practice at Monitor Company and subsequently became the standard process at P&G. Over the course of our careers, we worked to develop a robust framework around our strategic approach, a way to teach the concepts to others, and a methodology for bringing it to life in an organization. Within Monitor, Michael Porter, Mark Fuller,

Sandi Pocharski, and Jonathan Goodman played important roles in advancing this thinking. At P&G, Tom Laco, Steve Donovan, Clayt Daley, Gil Cloyd, and dozens of other business and functional leaders (including those whose stories are told in this book) all contributed substantially to the work of sharpening the strategy of the company. Along with Michael Porter, academics Peter Drucker and Chris Argyris were seminal influences who shaped our thinking and work.

Ultimately, this is a story about choices, including the choice to create a discipline of strategic thinking and strategic practice within an organization. Though we use P&G as our main example, this doesn't mean that our approach to strategy can only be effective in a global consumer goods company. We've seen it powerfully used in all manner of industries and all sizes of organizations, including start-ups, not-for-profits, and government agencies. But it was at P&G that we were really able to use this approach across a wide range of businesses, geographies, and functions and over a decade (and to see where it worked and didn't work)—so that is the story we have chosen to tell. We will use P&G brand, category, sector, function, and company examples to illustrate the strategy concepts and tools throughout the book. Of course, not all companies look like P&G. But it is our hope that through examples from across P&G's diverse businesses, organizations, and levels, the lessons for your organization will become clear.

What Is Strategy?

Strategy is a relatively young discipline. Until the middle of the last century, much of what people now think of as strategy was categorized simply as management. So it is really no wonder that many organizations struggle to define what a strategy is and how to create a useful one; there is no single, clear, and pervasive definition of strategy and even less consensus on how to build one. When a strategy succeeds, it seems a little like magic, unknowable and unexplainable in advance but obvious in retrospect.

It isn't. Really, strategy is about making specific choices to win in the marketplace. According to Mike Porter, author of *Competitive Strategy*, perhaps the most widely respected book on strategy ever written, a firm creates a sustainable competitive advantage over its rivals by "deliberately choosing a different set of activities to deliver unique value."[1] Strategy therefore requires making explicit choices—to do some things and not others—and building a business around those choices.[2] In short, strategy is choice. More specifically, *strategy is an integrated set of choices that uniquely positions the firm in its industry so as to create sustainable advantage and superior value relative to the competition.*

Making choices is hard work, and it doesn't always fit with all the other work to be done. In our view, far too few companies have a clear, choiceful, and compelling winning strategy in place. Too often, CEOs in particular will allow what is urgent to crowd out what is really important. When an organizational bias for action drives *doing*, often *thinking* falls by the wayside. Instead of working to develop a winning strategy, many leaders tend to approach strategy in one of the following ineffective ways:

1. *They define strategy as a vision.* Mission and vision statements are elements of strategy, but they aren't enough. They offer no guide to productive action and no explicit road map to the desired future. They don't include choices about what businesses to be in and not to be in. There's no focus on sustainable competitive advantage or the building blocks of value creation.

2. *They define strategy as a plan.* Plans and tactics are also elements of strategy, but they aren't enough either.

A detailed plan that specifies what the firm will do (and when) does not imply that the things it will do add up to sustainable competitive advantage.

3. *They deny that long-term (or even medium-term) strategy is possible.* The world is changing so quickly, some leaders argue, that it's impossible to think about strategy in advance and that, instead, a firm should respond to new threats and opportunities as they emerge. Emergent strategy has become the battle cry of many technology firms and start-ups, which do indeed face a rapidly changing marketplace. Unfortunately, such an approach places a company in a reactive mode, making it easy prey for more-strategic rivals. Not only is strategy possible in times of tumultuous change, but it can be a competitive advantage and a source of significant value creation. Is Apple disinclined to think about strategy? Is Google? Is Microsoft?

4. *They define strategy as the optimization of the status quo.* Many leaders try to optimize what they are already doing in their current business. This can create efficiency and drive some value. But it isn't strategy. The optimization of current practices does not address the very real possibility that the firm could be exhausting its assets and resources by optimizing the wrong activities, while more-strategic competitors pass it by. Think of legacy airlines optimizing their spoke-and-hub models while Southwest Airlines created a transformative new point-to-point business model. Optimization has a place in business, but it isn't strategy.

5. *They define strategy as following best practices.* Every industry has tools and practices that become widespread

and generic. Some organizations define strategy as benchmarking against competition and then doing the same set of activities but more effectively. Sameness isn't strategy. It is a recipe for mediocrity.

These ineffective approaches are driven by a misconception of what strategy really is and a reluctance to make truly hard choices. It is natural to want to keep options open as long as possible, rather than closing off possibilities by making explicit choices. But it is only through making and acting on choices that you can win. Yes, clear, tough choices force your hand and confine you to a path. But they also free you to focus on what matters.

What matters is winning. Great organizations—whether companies, not-for-profits, political organizations, agencies, what have you—choose to win rather than simply play. What is the difference between the Mayo Clinic and the average research hospital in your neighborhood? Your local hospital is, most likely, focused on providing a service and on doing good. The Mayo Clinic, though, sets out to transform the world of medicine, to be at the vanguard of medical research, and to win. And it does.

The Playbook: Five Choices, One Framework, One Process

Winning should be at the heart of any strategy. In our terms, *a strategy is a coordinated and integrated set of five choices: a winning aspiration, where to play, how to win, core capabilities, and management systems.* Chapter 1 introduces these five essential choices as strategic questions. Each of chapters 2 through 6 dwells at some length on one of the questions, explaining the nature of the choice to be made, providing a number of examples of that choice, and offering some advice for making the choice in your own context.

The five choices make up the *strategic choice cascade*, the foundation of our strategy work and the core of this book.

To really think through strategy, though, the cascade isn't quite enough. In chapter 7, we will provide another tool—the *strategy logic flow*, a framework designed to helpfully direct your thinking to the key analyses that inform your five strategy choices. Then, in chapter 8, we provide a specific methodology for making sense of conflicting strategic options, a process—called *reverse engineering*—for making strategic choices with others. Taken together, the five choices, one framework, and one process provide a playbook for crafting strategy in any organization.

Our intent is to provide you with a do-it-yourself guide to strategy. We offer you the concepts, process, and practical tools you need to create and develop a winning strategy for your business, function, or organization—a strategy that serves your customers better and enables you to compete more successfully and to win.

The world needs more business leaders who understand strategy and are capable of leading the strategy process for their companies. It needs strategic capabilities at all organizational levels in industries of all kinds, in government, in health care, in education, and in the social sector. Strategy needn't be mysterious. Conceptually, it is simple and straightforward. It requires clear and hard thinking, real creativity, courage, and personal leadership. But it can be done.

Chapter One

Strategy Is Choice

By the late 1990s it became clear that P&G really needed to win in skin care. Skin care (including soaps, cleansers, moisturizers, lotions, and other treatments) constitutes about a quarter of the total beauty industry and has the potential to be highly profitable. When done well, it can engender intense consumer loyalty compared with other beauty categories like hair care, cosmetics, and fragrances.[1] Plus, there's significant knowledge and skill transfer from skin care to these other categories in terms of technology and consumer insights. To be a credible player in the beauty business, P&G needed leading hair-care and skin-care brands. Skin care was the weak link. In particular, Oil of Olay was struggling. It wasn't P&G's only skin-care brand, but it was by far the largest and best known.

Unfortunately, the brand had baggage. Oil of Olay was seen as old-fashioned and no longer relevant. It had come to be derisively called "Oil of Old Lady," a not entirely unfair characterization, as its customer base was growing older every year. More and more, when selecting a skin-care regimen, women were passing over Oil of Olay in favor of brands with more to offer. Oil of Olay's core product (pink cream in a simple plastic bottle), sold mainly through drugstores at the bargain-basement price of $3.99, just wasn't competitive against an ever-growing range of skin-care alternatives. By the late 1990s, Oil of Olay sales were clocking in below $800 million a year, nowhere close to the industry leaders in the $50 billion skin-care category.

All this presented a difficult strategic choice and generated a number of possible responses. P&G could maintain status quo on Oil of Olay and launch a more relevant alternative under a different brand name to compete for a new generation of consumers. But building a skin-care brand from scratch to market leadership could take years, even decades. P&G could go for an immediate fix, buying an established skin-care leader (think Estée Lauder's Clinique or Beiersdorf's Nivea brand) to more credibly compete in the category. But an acquisition would be both expensive and speculative. Plus, over the previous decade, P&G had actively pursued several opportunities for leading brands with no success. P&G could attempt to extend one of its leading beauty brands, like Cover Girl, into the skin-care category. This too would be highly speculative. How easily could even a leading cosmetics brand gain traction in skin care? Finally, P&G could attempt to revive a fading but still valuable Oil of Olay to compete in a new segment. This meant finding a way to reinvent the brand in the minds of consumers, a big investment with no guarantee of success. But P&G believed that the Oil of Olay brand had potential, especially with the right push behind it.

The good news was that there was still widespread consumer awareness of Oil of Olay, and as every good marketer knows, awareness precedes trial. Michael Kuremsky, Oil of Olay's North American brand manager at the time, summed up the state of affairs: "There was still a lot of promise. [But] there was really no plan."[2] The team wanted to turn the promise into a plan. The plan was to remake Oil of Olay—its brand, its business model, its package and product, its value proposition, and even its name. Out went "Oil of," and the brand was rechristened "Olay."[3]

Rethinking Olay

Together with Susan Arnold, then president of global beauty, we focused on the mid- and long-term strategy for beauty, working to establish P&G as a credible contender in the sector. As P&G learned the beauty game, it could win across the categories. So, P&G invested in the SK-II brand (a super-premium Japanese skin-care line acquired when P&G bought Max Factor in 1991), Cover Girl (P&G's leading cosmetics brand), Pantene (its biggest shampoo and conditioner brand), Head & Shoulders (its leading anti-dandruff shampoo line), and Herbal Essences (its hair-care brand aimed at a younger demographic). The company bought Wella and Clairol, to create a position in hair styling and color. And it pursued acquisitions that could build leadership in skin care. The Olay team, meanwhile, worked to reinvent the brand.

Led by Gina Drosos (then general manager for the skin-care business), the team set to work to understand its consumers and its competition. The team members discovered, to no one's surprise, that Olay's existing customers were price sensitive and only minimally invested in skin care. Conventional wisdom was that the most attractive consumer segment was women aged fifty-plus and concerned with fighting wrinkles. These women would pay significant premiums for promising products, and this was where the leading brands tended to focus. But, Drosos recalls, "We found, as we looked at consumer needs in the market, that there was real growth potential with consumers who were thirty-five-plus, when they noticed their first lines and wrinkles. Before that, a lot of women were still using hand and body lotions on their face or really nothing at all."[4] The midthirties seemed to be a potential point of entry in women's skin care. At this age, consumers become more aware of, and committed to, a regimen—cleansing, toning, and moisturizing and using day creams, night creams, weekly facials, and other treatments to keep the appearance of youthful, healthy skin. In their midthirties, women tend to become more highly committed to skin care and are more willing to pay for quality and innovation. They seek out a preferred brand on a regular basis and try new offerings from it. They become loyal devotees. These were the consumers Olay needed, but to play in this segment, Olay would have to up its game significantly.

Traditionally in the beauty industry, department store brands have taken the lead on innovation, developing new products and better products that, over time, trickle down to the mass market. Given P&G's greater scale, lower distribution costs, and considerable in-house R&D capabilities, there was an opportunity to lead on innovation from the middle of the market. "We could flip this consumer paradigm that the best technology trickles down," Drosos says. "We could have the best technology come from Olay." So, P&G scientists went to work on sourcing and developing better and more-effective compounds—skin-care products that could dramatically outperform existing products in the market. Rather than focus exclusively on wrinkles as a product benefit, Olay broadened the value proposition.

The research showed that wrinkles were but one of many concerns. Joe Listro, Olay's R&D vice president, notes, "Besides wrinkles, there was dry skin, age spots, and uneven skin tone problems. Consumers were telling us, 'We have these other needs.' We were working on technologies from a skin-biology and noticeable-appearance standpoint. We identified a material combination called VitaNiacin that showed noticeable benefits across a range of these factors that could actually improve the appearance of skin."[5] Olay sought to redefine what anti-aging products could do. The result was a series of new products, beginning with Olay Total Effects in 1999, that combined consumer insights with better active ingredients to fight the multiple signs of aging. The products marked a significant improvement in skin-care performance for consumers.

The new, more effective products could credibly be sold in departments stores like Macy's and Saks, the *prestige channel* that accounted for more than half of the market. Olay had traditionally been sold only in the mass channel, through drugstores and discount retailers. These mass retailers, including Walgreens, Target, and Walmart, were P&G's biggest and best customers across multiple categories. But the company had precious little experience in, and influence with, department stores, where it sold in just a few categories. To play to P&G's strengths, it made sense to stay in mass channels, but only if department store consumers would defect there for Olay. To win with Olay in mass, the company had to bridge the mass and prestige markets, creating what it would come to call a *masstige* category. Olay needed to shift the perception of beauty care in the mass channel, selling higher-end, more prestigious products in a traditionally high-volume environment. It needed to attract consumers from both the mass and the prestige channels. To do so, the product itself was only a part of the battle; Olay also needed to shift consumer perception of the brand and channel through its positioning, packaging, pricing, and promotions.

First, Olay needed to convince skin-care-savvy women that the new Olay products were just as good as, or better than, higher-priced competitors. It began with advertising in the same magazines and on the same television shows as those populated by the more expensive brands; the idea was to put Olay into the same category in the consumer's mind. Ads highlighted Olay as the way to fight "the seven signs of aging," and outside experts were enlisted to bolster claims relating to the new and better ingredients.

Drosos explains, "We developed a breakthrough external-relations and credentialing program. We determined who would be the key influencers for consumers. We opened our labs to some of the top dermatologists to come in to see the work we were doing." Independent tests, which showed Olay products performing as well as or better than department store brands costing hundreds of dollars more, helped reframe consumer perceptions of performance and value. All of a sudden, Olay was seen as offering high-quality products at an affordable price.

Olay also needed to look the part. The packaging had to represent an aspiration, but also effectively deliver the product. Recalls Listro, "Most products in mass, and even prestige to some extent, were sold either in squeeze bottles or in generic jars. What we were looking for was a technology that could deliver a thick cream elegantly, more like a lotion. We found this design that could actually pump creams." The result: a package that would look distinctive and impressive on the shelf, but also work effectively once the product was at home.

Pricing was the next element. Traditionally, Olay products had sold, like most drugstore brands, in the sub-$8 price category (compared with department store brands, which could be priced anywhere from $25 to $400 or more). As Drosos explains, in skin care, there was the pervasive belief "that you get what you pay for. Women felt the products available in the mass-market channel were just not as good." Olay's advertising and packaging promised a high-quality, effective product that could compete with department store brands. Its pricing needed to hit the perfect note as well—not so high that mass consumers would be turned off, but not so low that prestige consumers would doubt its efficacy (no matter what those independent experts said).

Listro recalls the testing that went on to determine the pricing strategy for Olay Total Effects: "We started to test the new

Olay product at premium price points of $12.99 to $18.99 and got very different results at those price points." At $12.99, there was a positive response and a reasonably good rate of purchase intent (a stated intention to buy the product in the future). But most of the subjects who signaled a desire to buy at $12.99 were mass shoppers. Very few department store shoppers were interested at that price point. "Basically," explains Listro, "we were trading people up from within the channel." That was good, but not enough. At $15.99, purchase intent dropped considerably. Then, at $18.99, purchase intent went back up again—way up. "So, $12.99 was really good, $15.99 not so good, $18.99 great. We found that at $18.99, we were starting to get consumers who would shop in both channels. At $18.99, it was a great value to a prestige shopper who was used to spending $30 or more." The $18.99 price point was just below Clinique and considerably below Estée Lauder. For the prestige shopper, it was great value, but not too cheap to be credible. And for the mass shopper, it signified that the product must be considerably better than anything else on the shelf to justify such a premium. Listro continues: "But $15.99 was no-man's-land—way too expensive for a mass shopper and really not credible enough for a prestige shopper." So, with a strong push from the senior leadership team, Olay took the leap to $18.99 for the launch of Olay Total Effects. It was set as the manufacturer suggested retail price, and the team worked hard to convince retailers to stick to that price.

Momentum started to build. Olay followed up with an even more expensive premium brand, with a yet-better active ingredient: Olay Regenerist. Then, it introduced Olay Definity and then the still-higher premium Olay Pro-X—which sold at a $50 price point, something inconceivable ten years earlier. The team built and deepened capabilities around the new strategy. For most of the 1990s, P&G's skin-care business had grown at 2 to 4 percent per year. Following the 2000 relaunch, Olay had double-digit sales and profit growth every year for the next decade. The result: a $2.5 billion brand with extremely high margins and a consumer base squarely in the heart of the most attractive part of the market.

What Strategy Is (and Isn't)

Olay had a strategic problem that many companies struggle with—a stagnant brand, aging consumers, uncompetitive products, strong competition, and momentum in the wrong direction. So, why was Olay able to succeed spectacularly where so many fail? The people at Olay aren't harder working, more dedicated, bolder, or luckier than everyone else. But their way of thinking about the choices they made was different. They had a clear and defined approach to strategy, a thinking process that enabled individual managers to effectively make clearer and harder choices. That process, and the approach to strategy that underpins it, is what made the difference.

Strategy can seem mystical and mysterious. It isn't. It is easily defined. It is a set of choices about winning. Again, it is an integrated set of choices that uniquely positions the firm in its industry so as to create sustainable advantage and superior value relative to the competition. Specifically, strategy is the answer to these five interrelated questions:

1. *What is your winning aspiration?* The purpose of your enterprise, its motivating aspiration.

2. *Where will you play?* A playing field where you can achieve that aspiration.

3. *How will you win?* The way you will win on the chosen playing field.

4. *What capabilities must be in place?* The set and configuration of capabilities required to win in the chosen way.

5. *What management systems are required?* The systems and measures that enable the capabilities and support the choices.

These choices and the relationship between them can be understood as a reinforcing cascade, with the choices at the top of the cascade setting the context for the choices below, and choices at the bottom influencing and refining the choices above (figure 1-1).

In a small organization, there may well be a single choice cascade that defines the set of choices for the entire organization. But in larger companies, there are multiple levels of choices and interconnected cascades. At P&G, for instance, there is a brand-level

FIGURE 1-1

An integrated cascade of choices

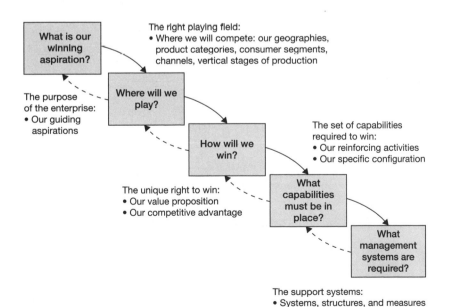

What is our winning aspiration?

The right playing field:
• Where we will compete: our geographies, product categories, consumer segments, channels, vertical stages of production

The purpose of the enterprise:
• Our guiding aspirations

Where will we play?

The set of capabilities required to win:
• Our reinforcing activities
• Our specific configuration

How will we win?

The unique right to win:
• Our value proposition
• Our competitive advantage

What capabilities must be in place?

What management systems are required?

The support systems:
• Systems, structures, and measures required to support our choices

strategy that articulates the five choices for a brand such as Olay or Pampers. There is a category strategy that covers multiple related brands, like skin care or diapers. There is a sector strategy that covers multiple categories, for example, beauty or baby care. And finally, there is a strategy at the company level, too. Each strategy influences and is influenced by the choices above and below it; company-level where-to-play choices, for instance, guide choices at the sector level, which in turn affect the category-level and brand-level choices. And the brand-level choices influence the category-level choices, which influence the sector- and company-level choices. The result is a set of nested cascades that cover the full organization (figure 1-2).

The nested cascades mean that choices happen at every level of the organization. Consider a company that designs, manufactures, and sells yoga apparel. It aspires to create fierce brand advocates, to make a difference in the world, and to make money doing it.

FIGURE 1-2

Nested choice cascades

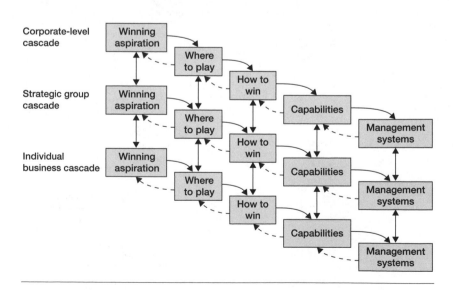

It chooses to play in its own retail stores, with athletic wear for women. It decides to win on the basis of performance and style. It creates yoga gear that is both technically superior (in terms of fit, flex, wear, moisture wicking, etc.) and utterly cool. It turns over its stock frequently to create a feeling of exclusivity and scarcity. It draws customers into the store with staff members who have deep expertise. It defines a number of capabilities essential to winning, like product and store design, customer service, and supply-chain expertise. It creates sourcing and design processes, training systems for staff, and logistics management systems. All of these choices are made at the top of the organization.

But these choices beget more choices in the rest of the organization. Should the product team stay only in clothing or expand to accessories? Should it play in menswear as well? Should the retail operations group stay in bricks and mortar or expand online? Within retail, should there be one store model or several to adapt to different geographies and customer segments? At the store level, how should the staff person serve the customer, here and now, in order to win? Each level in the organization has its own strategic choice cascade.

Consider the salesperson in the Manhattan store. She defines winning as being the best salesperson in the store and having customers who are delighted with her service. From not only her daily sales numbers but also her interactions with repeat customers and feedback from her peers, she knows she's succeeding. Her where-to-play choice is largely defined by the folks who walk in the door, but she may notice that there are types of customers, times of day, or parts of the store where she can best bring her skills to bear. She consequently turns her attention there. In terms of how to win, she may have one approach for customers who are new to yoga and intimidated by all the choices (offering advice not just on attire but on how to get started, as well as reassurance that it will all make sense in time), another for aficionados (highlighting the technical specs of the gear but also swapping stories about classes and instructors), and another for the fashion crowd who seek yoga pants not for athletics but for running errands (pointing out racks of new arrivals, emphasizing unique colors and designs). She chooses to develop her own capabilities in clear communication, understanding technical specs, and practicing different forms of yoga. She builds her own management systems, like a personal cheat sheet for products and styles and a directory of her favorite local studios and instructors.

These frontline choices may not seem as complex as the choices facing the CEO, but they are indeed strategic choices. Like the CEO, a salesperson must make the best choices she can under constraints and uncertainty. Her constraints came from the choices made above her in the organization, from the demands of her customers, and from the strategies of her competitors. For the CEO, the constraints came from the expectations of the capital markets, the company's cash reserves, and the directions of the board of directors. Both the salesperson and her CEO are making strategic choices and acting upon them—the only difference is the scope of the choices and the precise nature of the constraints.

Strategy can be created and refined at every level of the organization using the choice cascade framework. Each box of the choice cascade is the subject of an upcoming chapter, but for now, we'll explain a little about each one, using Olay brand-level and P&G company-level choices as illustrations.

Winning Aspirations

The first question—what is our winning aspiration?—sets the frame for all the other choices. A company must seek to win in a particular place and in a particular way. If it doesn't seek to win, it is wasting the time of its people and the investments of its capital providers. But to be most helpful, the abstract concept of winning should be translated into defined aspirations. Aspirations are statements about the ideal future. At a later stage in the process, a company ties to those aspirations some specific benchmarks that measure progress toward them.

At Olay, the winning aspirations were defined as market share leadership in North America, $1 billion in sales, and a global share that put the brand among the market leaders. A revitalized and transformed Olay was expected to establish skin care as a strong pillar for beauty along with hair care. Establishing and maintaining leadership of a new masstige segment, positioned between mass and prestige, was a third aspiration. This set of aspirations served as a starting point to define where to play and how to win, enabling the Olay team to see the larger purpose in what it was doing. Clarity about the winning aspirations meant that actions at the brand, category, sector, and company level were directed at delivering against that ideal.

At the overall company level, winning was defined as delivering the most valuable, value-creating brands in every category and industry in which P&G chose to compete (in other words, market leadership in all of P&G's categories). The aspiration was to create sustainable competitive advantage, superior value, and superior financial returns. P&G's statement of purpose, at the time, read as follows: "We will provide products and services of superior quality and value that improve the lives of the world's consumers. As a result, consumers will reward us with leadership sales, profit and value creation, allowing our people, our shareholders, and the communities in which we live and work to prosper." Improving consumers' lives to drive leadership sales, profit, and value creation was the company's most important aspiration. It drove all subsequent choices.

Aspirations can be refined and revised over time. However, aspirations shouldn't change day to day; they exist to consistently align activities within the firm, so should be designed to last for some time. A definition of winning provides a context for the rest of the strategic choices; in all cases, choices should fit within and support the firm's aspirations. The question of what a winning aspiration is will be further explored in chapter 2.

Where to Play

The next two questions are where to play and how to win. These two choices, which are tightly bound up with one another, form the very heart of strategy and are the two most critical questions in strategy formulation. The winning aspiration broadly defines the scope of the firm's activities; where to play and how to win define the specific activities of the organization—what the firm will do, and where and how it will do this, to achieve its aspirations.

Where to play represents the set of choices that narrow the competitive field. The questions to be asked focus on where the company will compete—in which markets, with which customers and consumers, in which channels, in which product categories, and at which vertical stage or stages of the industry in question. This set of questions is vital; no company can be all things to all people and still win, so it is important to understand which where-to-play choices will best enable the company to win. A firm can be narrow or broad. It can compete in any number of demographic segments (men ages eighteen to twenty-four, midlife urbanites, working moms) and geographies (local, national, international, developed world, economically fast-advancing countries like Brazil and China). It can compete in myriad services, product lines, and categories. It can participate in different channels (direct to consumer, online, mass merchandise, grocery, department store).

It can participate in the upstream part of its industry, downstream, or be vertically integrated. These choices, when taken together, capture the strategic playing field for the firm.

Olay made two strategically decisive where-to-play choices: to create, with retail partners, a new masstige segment in mass discount stores, drugstores, and grocery stores to compete with prestige brands and to develop a new and growing point-of-entry consumer segment for anti-aging skin-care products. Many other where-to-play options were considered (like moving into prestige channels and selling through department and specialty stores), but to win, Olay's choices on where to play needed to make sense in light of P&G's company-level where-to-play choices and capabilities. P&G tends to do well when the consumer is highly involved with the product category and cares a good deal about product experience and performance. It excels with brands that promise real improvement when the consumer puts in effort on a regular basis, as part of a well-defined regimen. P&G also does well with brands that can be sold through its best customers, retailers with which it has strong relationships and with which it can create significant shared value. So, the Olay team decided where to play with the P&G choices and capabilities in mind.

Corporately, when it came to where to play, the company needed to define which regions, categories, channels, and consumers would give P&G a sustainable competitive advantage. The idea was to play in those areas where P&G's capabilities would be decisive and to avoid areas where they were not. The concept that helped P&G leaders sort one area from the other and to define the strategic playing field clearly was the idea of *core*.

We wanted to play where P&G's core strengths would enable it to win. We asked which brands truly were core brands, identifying a set of brands that were clear industry or category leaders and devoting resources to them disproportionately. We asked what P&G's core geographies were. With ten countries representing 85 percent of profits, P&G had to focus on winning in those countries. We asked where consumers expected P&G brands and products to be sold, that is, mass merchandisers and discounters, drugstores, and grocery stores. Core became a theme in innovation as well. P&G scientists determined the core technologies that were important across the businesses and focused on those technologies above all others. We wanted to shift from a pure invention mind-set to one of strategic innovation; the goal was innovation that drove the core. Core consumers were a theme too; we pushed businesses to focus on the consumer who matters most, targeting the most attractive consumer segments. Core was the first and most fundamental where-to-play choice—to focus on core brands, geographies, channels, technologies, and consumers as a platform for growth.

The second where-to-play choice was to extend P&G's core into demographically advantaged and structurally more attractive categories. For example, the core was to move from fabric into home care, from hair care into hair color and styling, and more broadly into beauty, health, and personal care.

The third where-to-play choice—to expand into emerging markets—was driven by demographics and economics. The majority of babies would be born, and households formed, in emerging markets. Economic growth in these markets will be as much as four times as high as in the OECD (Organisation for Economic Co-operation and Development) developed markets. The question was how many markets P&G could take on and in what priority order. The company started with China, Mexico, and Russia, building capability and reach over time to include Brazil, India, and others. As Chip Bergh, former group president for global grooming and now CEO of Levi Strauss & Co., notes, "In 2000, about 20 percent of P&G's total sales were in emerging markets compared to Unilever and Colgate, which were already up near 40 percent. We were a company of premium-priced products, always going after product superiority. We tended to play, as a company, in the premium tiers in almost all categories."[6] To compete in the developing world, Bergh says, a change in orientation was required: "We needed to begin broadening our portfolio and developing competitive propositions, including cost structures that would allow us to reach deeper into these emerging markets. There are a billion consumers in India, and we were reaching the top 10 percent of them."

Emerging markets would be an important where-to-play choice, but not all emerging markets all at once. China and Russia represented unique opportunities, as their markets opened to all comers at the same time. P&G had focused on these countries first and established strong, strategic leading positions in both markets. Now, the company thought hard about which emerging markets to target next, and with which products and categories. Baby care in Asia, for instance, made great sense—since, for the foreseeable future, most of the world's babies would be born in Asia. Laundry and beauty also made sense in emerging markets, for reasons of brand equity, scale, and consumer preference. So, P&G sought to make inroads in Asia, in those three categories, and it did. By 2011, 35 percent of total sales came from the developing world.

In sum, there were three critical where-to-play choices for P&G at the corporate level:

- Grow in and from the core businesses, focusing on core consumer segments, channels, customers, geographies, brands, and product technologies.

- Extend leadership in laundry and home care, and build to market leadership in the more demographically advantaged and structurally attractive beauty and personal-care categories.

- Expand to leadership in demographically advantaged emerging markets, prioritizing markets by their strategic importance to P&G.

In chapter 3, we'll return to the question of where to play, exploring the different ways to define your playing field and the lessons that can be learned from brands like Bounty and Tide.

How to Win

Where to play selects the playing field; how to win defines the choices for winning on that field. It is the recipe for success in the chosen segments, categories, channels, geographies, and so on. The how-to-win choice is intimately tied to the where-to-play choice. Remember, it is not how to win generally, but how to win within the chosen where-to-play domains.

The where-to-play and how-to-win choices should flow from and reinforce one another. Think of the contrast between two kinds of restaurant empires—say, Olive Garden versus Mario Batali. Both specialize in Italian food, and both are successful across multiple locations. But they represent very different where-to-play choices.

Olive Garden is a midpriced, casual dining chain with considerable scale—more than seven hundred restaurants around the world. As a result, its how-to-win choices relate to meeting the needs of average diners and focus on achieving reliable, consistent outcomes when hiring thousands of employees to reproduce millions of meals that will suit a wide array of tastes. Mario Batali, on the other hand, competes at the very high end of the fine-dining space and does so in just a few places—New York, Las Vegas, Los Angeles, and Singapore. He wins by designing innovative and exciting recipes; sourcing the very best of ingredients; delivering superlative, customized service; and sharing his cachet with his foodie patrons—cachet generated by Batali's Food Network celebrity and friendships with the likes of actress Gwyneth Paltrow.

In great strategies, the where-to-play and how-to-win choices fit together to make the company stronger. Given their where-to-play choices, it would not make sense for Olive Garden to try to win by increasing the celebrity status of its head chef, nor for Batali to even contemplate making each location look just like the others. But if Batali wanted to seriously expand to a lower-priced, casual dining range, as Wolfgang Puck has done, Batali would need to expand his how-to-win choices to fit the new, broader where-to-play choice. If he failed to do so, he would likely fail to engage the new market. Where-to-play and how-to-win choices must be considered together, because no how-to-win is perfect, or even appropriate, for all where-to-play choices.

To determine how to win, an organization must decide what will enable it to create unique value and sustainably deliver that value to customers in a way that is distinct from the firm's competitors. Michael Porter called it competitive advantage—the specific way a firm utilizes its advantages to create superior value for a consumer or a customer and in turn, superior returns for the firm.

For Olay, the how-to-win choices were to formulate genuinely better skin-care products that could actually fight the signs of aging, to create a powerful marketing campaign that clearly articulated the brand promise ("Fight the Seven Signs of Aging"), and to establish a masstige channel, working with mass retailers to compete directly with prestige brands. The masstige choice, which was a decision to win in the channels P&G knew best, required significant changes in product formulation, package design, branding, and pricing to reframe the value proposition for retailers and consumers.

Corporately, P&G chose to compete from the core; to extend into home, beauty, health, and personal care; and to expand into emerging markets. The how-to-win choices needed to work optimally with these where-to-play choices. To be successful, how-to-win choices should be suited to the specific context of the firm in question and highly difficult for competitors to copy. P&G's competitive advantages are its ability to understand its core consumers and to create differentiated brands. It wins by relentlessly building its brands and through innovative product technology. It leverages global scale and strong partnerships with suppliers and channel customers to deliver strong retail distribution and consumer value in its chosen markets. If P&G played to its strengths and invested in them, it could sustain competitive advantage through a unique go-to-market model.

P&G's where-to-play and how-to-win-choices aren't appropriate for every context. The key to making the right choices for your business is that they must be doable and decisive for you. If you are a small entrepreneurial firm facing much larger competitors, making a how-to-win choice on the basis of scale would not make much sense. But simply because you are small doesn't mean winning through scale is impossible. Don't dismiss the possibility that you can change the context to fit your choices. Bob Young, cofounder of Red Hat, Inc., knew precisely where he wanted his company to play: he wanted to serve corporate customers with open-source enterprise software. In his view, the how-to-win in that context required scale—Young saw that corporate customers were much more likely to buy from a market leader, especially a dominant market leader. At the time, the Linux market was highly fragmented, with no such clear leader. Young had to change the game—by literally giving his software away via free download—to achieve dominant market share and become credible to corporate information technology (IT) departments. In that case, Young decided where to play and how to win, and then built the rest of his strategy (earning revenue from service rather than software sales) around these two choices. The result was a billion-dollar company with a thriving enterprise business.

The myriad ways to win, and possibilities for thinking through them, will be explored in greater depth in chapter 4. There, we begin with the story of a set of technologies that posed a particularly challenging how-to-win choice for P&G.

Core Capabilities

Two questions flow from and support the heart of strategy: (1) what capabilities must be in place to win, and (2) what management systems are required to support the strategic choices? The first of these questions, the capabilities choice, relates to the range and quality of activities that will enable a company to win where it chooses to play. Capabilities are the map of activities and competencies that critically underpin specific where-to-play and how-to-win choices.

The Olay team had to invest in building and creating its capabilities on a number of fronts: clearly, innovation would be vital—and not just product innovation—but packaging, distribution, marketing, and even business model innovation would play a role. The team would need to leverage its existing consumer insights to truly understand a different segment. It would have to build the brand, advertise, and merchandise with mass retailers in new ways. Olay and P&G skin care couldn't go it alone. So, they partnered with product ingredient innovators (Cellderma), designers (IDEO and others), advertising and PR agencies (Saatchi & Saatchi), and key influencers (like beauty magazine editors and dermatologists, for credible product performance endorsements). This networked alliance of internal and external capabilities created a unique and powerful activity system. It required deepening existing capabilities and building new ones.

At P&G, a company with more than 125,000 employees worldwide, the range of capabilities is broad and diverse. But only a few capabilities are absolutely fundamental to winning in the places and manner that it has chosen:

Deep consumer understanding. This is the ability to truly know shoppers and end users. The goal is to uncover the unarticulated needs of consumers, to know consumers better than any competitors do, and to see opportunities before they are obvious to others.

Innovation. Innovation is P&G's lifeblood. P&G seeks to translate deep understanding of consumer needs into new and continuously improved products. Innovation efforts may be applied to the product, to the packaging, to the way P&G serves its consumers and works with its trade customers, or even to its business models, core capabilities, and management systems.

Brand building. Branding has long been one of P&G's strongest capabilities. By better defining and distilling a brand-building heuristic, P&G can train and develop brand leaders and marketers in this discipline effectively and efficiently.

Go-to-market ability. This capability concerns channel and consumer relationships. P&G thrives on reaching its customers and consumers at the right time, in the right place, in the right way. By investing in unique partnerships with retailers, P&G can create new and breakthrough go-to-market strategies that allow it to deliver more value to consumers in the store and to retailers throughout the supply chain.

Global scale. P&G is a global, multicategory company. Rather than operate in distinct silos, its categories can increase the power of the whole by hiring together, learning together, buying together, researching and testing together, and going to market together. In the 1990s, P&G amalgamated a whole suite of internal support services, like employee services and IT, under one umbrella—global business services (GBS)—to allow it to capture the scale benefits of those functions globally.

These five core capabilities support and reinforce one another and, taken together, set P&G apart. In isolation, each capability is strong, but insufficient to generate true competitive advantage over the long term. Rather, the way all of them work together and reinforce each other is what generates enduring advantage. A great new idea coming out of P&G labs can be effectively branded and shelved around the world in the best retail outlets in each market. That combination is hard for competitors to match. Core capabilities, and the way in which they relate to competitive advantage, will be discussed further in chapter 5.

Management Systems

The final strategic choice in the cascade focuses on management systems. These are the systems that foster, support, and measure the strategy. To be truly effective, they must be purposefully designed to support the choices and capabilities. The types of systems and measures will vary from choice to choice, capability to capability, and company to company. In general, though, the systems need to ensure that choices are communicated to the whole company, employees are trained to deliver on choices and leverage capabilities, plans are made to invest in and sustain capabilities over time, and the efficacy of the choices and progress toward aspirations are measured.

Beneath Olay's choices and capabilities, the team built supporting systems and measures that included a "love the job you're in" human resources strategy (to encourage personal development and deepen the talent pool in the beauty sector) and detailed tracking systems to measure consumer responses to brand, package, product lines, and every other element of the marketing mix. Olay organized around innovation, creating a structure wherein one team was working on the strategy and rollout of current products while another was designing the next generation. It developed technical marketers, individuals with expertise in R&D as well as marketing, who could speak credibly to dermatologists and beauty editors. It created systems to partner with leading in-store marketing and design firms, to create Olay displays that were eye-catching and inviting to shop. It also leveraged P&G systems like global purchasing, the global market development organization (MDO), and GBS so that individuals on the skin-care and Olay teams were freed up to focus where they added the most value.

At the corporate level, management systems included strategy dialogues, innovation-program reviews, brand-equity reviews, budget and operating plan discussions, and talent assessment development reviews. From the year 2000 on, every one of these management systems was changed significantly so that it became more effective. All of these systems were tightly integrated, mutually reinforcing, and crucial to winning. Management systems in general, and the way they work specifically at P&G, will be explored in greater depth in chapter 6.

The Power of Choices

We began this discussion with the Olay story. In our view, Olay succeeded because it had an integrated set of five strategic choices (figure 1-3) that fit beautifully with the choices of the corporate

FIGURE 1-3

Olay's choices

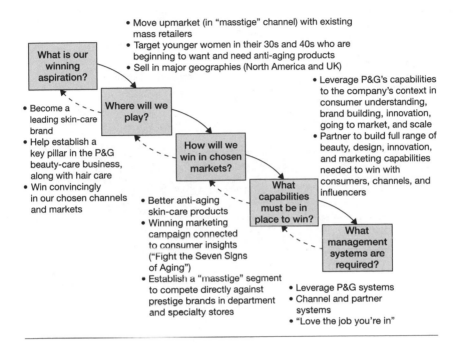

parent (figure 1-4). Because the choices were well integrated and reinforced category-, sector-, and company-level choices, succeeding at the Olay brand level actually helped deliver on the strategies above it.

Olay leveraged P&G's core capabilities in ways that made sense for the brand. The Olay team used deep consumer understanding to determine just where and how it could position Olay as an anti-aging powerhouse. It leveraged scale and R&D leadership to create a better product at a competitive price. It used P&G's brand-building expertise and channel relationships to convince consumers to try the product on the store shelves. All of this was crucial to reinventing the brand, to transforming its position in the marketplace, and to truly winning.

FIGURE 1-4

P&G's choices

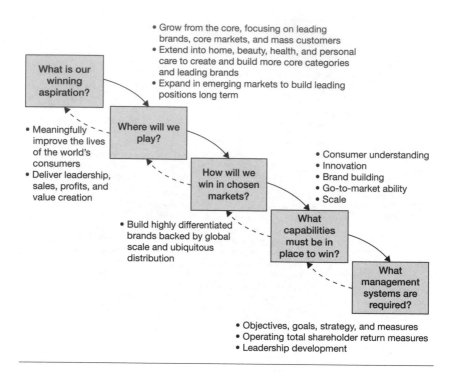

Summing Up

It isn't entirely easy to make your way through the full choice cascade. Doing so isn't a one-way, linear process. There is no checklist, whereby you create and articulate aspirations, then move on to where-to-play and how-to-win choices, then consider capabilities. Rather, strategy is an iterative process in which all of the moving parts influence one another and must be taken into account together. A company must understand its existing core capabilities and consider them when deciding where to play and how to win. But it may need to generate and invest in new core capabilities to support important, forward-looking where-to-play and how-to-win choices, too. Considering the dynamic feedback loop between all five choices, strategy isn't easy. But it is doable. A clear and powerful framework for thinking about choices is a helpful start for managers and other leaders intent on improving the strategy for their business or function.

Strategy needn't be the purview of a small set of experts. It can be demystified into a set of five important questions that can (and should) be asked at every level of the business: What is your winning aspiration? Where should you play? How can you win there? What capabilities do you need? What management systems would support it all? These choices, which can be understood as a strategic choice cascade, can be captured on a single page. They can create a shared understanding of your company's strategy and what must be done to achieve it. The essence of each choice and how to think about the choices (separately and together) will be the subject of the next five chapters, beginning with the first question: what is the winning aspiration?

CHOICE CASCADE DOS AND DON'TS

At the end of each chapter, we will share a few quick bits of advice—the things you should do or should avoid doing as you apply the lessons of the chapter to your own business.

- ✓ Do remember that strategy is about winning choices. It is a coordinated and integrated set of five very specific choices. As you define your strategy, choose what you will do and what you will not do.

- ✓ Do make your way through all five choices. Don't stop after defining winning, after choosing where to play and how to win, or even after assessing your capabilities. All five questions must be answered if you are to create a viable, actionable, and sustainable strategy.

✓ Do think of strategy as an iterative process; as you uncover insights at one stage in the cascade, you may well need to revisit choices elsewhere in the cascade.

✓ Do understand that strategy happens at multiple levels in the organization. An organization can be thought of as a set of nested cascades. Keep the other cascades in mind while working on yours.

✓ Do remember that there is no one perfect strategy; find the distinctive choices that work for you.

Chapter Two

What Is Winning

Aspirations are the guiding purpose of an enterprise. Think of the Starbucks mission statement: "To inspire and nurture the human spirit—one person, one cup, and one neighborhood at a time." Or Nike's: "To bring inspiration and innovation to every athlete* in the world." (The additional note, indicated by the asterisk, reads: "*If you have a body, you're an athlete.") And McDonald's: "Be our customers' favorite place and way to eat." Each is a statement of what the company seeks to be and a reflection of its reason to exist. But a lofty mission isn't a strategy. It is merely a starting point.

The first box in the strategic choice cascade—what is our winning aspiration?—defines the purpose of your enterprise, its guiding mission and aspiration, in strategic terms. What does winning look like for this organization? What, specifically, is its strategic aspiration? These answers are the foundation of your discussion of strategy; they set the context for all the strategic choices that follow.

There are many ways the higher-order aspiration of a company can be expressed. As a rule of thumb, though, start with people (consumers and customers) rather than money (stock price).

Peter Drucker argued that the purpose of an organization is to create a customer, and it's still true today. Consider the mission statements noted above. Starbucks, Nike, and McDonald's, each massively successful in its own way, frame their ambitions around their customers. And note the tenor of those aspirations: Nike wants to serve every athlete (not just some of them); McDonald's wants to be its customers' favorite place to eat (not just a convenient choice for families on the go). Each company doesn't just want to serve customers; it wants to win with them. And that is the single most crucial dimension of a company's aspiration: a company must play to win. To play merely to participate is self-defeating. It is a recipe for mediocrity. Winning is what matters—and it is the ultimate criterion of a successful strategy. Once the aspiration to win is set, the rest of the strategic questions relate directly to finding ways to deliver the win.

Why is it so important to make winning an explicit aspiration? Winning is worthwhile; a significant proportion (and often a disproportionate share) of industry value-creation accrues to the industry leader. But winning is also hard. It takes hard choices, dedicated effort, and substantial investment. Lots of companies try to win and still can't do it. So imagine, then, the likelihood of winning without explicitly setting out to do so. When a company sets out to participate, rather than win, it will inevitably fail to make the tough choices and the significant investments that would make winning even a remote possibility. A too-modest aspiration is far more dangerous than a too-lofty one. Too many companies eventually die a death of modest aspirations.

Playing to Play

Consider one of the costliest strategic gambles of the last century: General Motors' decision to launch Saturn. The context is important, of course. In the 1950s, at the end of legendary chairman

Alfred P. Sloan's tenure, GM had more employees than did any other company in the world and owned more than half of the US automotive market. It was the biggest of the Big Three and, for a time, the greatest and most powerful company on earth. But Sloan retired. Tastes changed, partly in response to the oil shocks of the 1970s. An incursion of cheaper, fuel-efficient imports began to make GM's lineup look old-fashioned and unaffordable.

By the 1980s, GM's core US brands—including Oldsmobile, Chevy, and Buick—were in decline. Younger car buyers were turning to Toyota, Honda, and Nissan, choosing these automakers' smaller and more economical models. Costs were a growing concern too; as GM's unionized workforce aged, generous retiree benefits contributed to higher and higher legacy costs—and those costs were passed on to car buyers. Meanwhile, relations with the United Auto Workers were poor and not getting any better, as GM restructured operations, closed plants, shifted resources, and laid off tens of thousands of workers.

In 1990, at a strategic crossroads, GM made a bold choice. It launched a new brand to compete in the small-car market. Saturn— "a different kind of company, a different kind of car"—would be GM's first new brand in almost seventy years, and it marked the first time GM would use a subsidiary, rather than a division, to make and sell cars. The goal, per then chairman Roger Smith, was to "sell a car at the lower end of the market and still make money."[1] In short, Saturn was GM's answer to the Japanese imports that threatened to dominate the small-car market; it was a defensive strategy, a way of playing in the small-car segment, designed to protect what remained of the ground GM was losing.

GM set up a separate Saturn head office. It negotiated a simplified, flexible deal with the United Auto Workers for Saturn's Spring Hill plant, guaranteeing workers greater control and profit sharing in exchange for lower base wages. Saturn also took a remarkably different approach to customer service, beginning with a no-haggle, one-price policy at all its dealerships. At Saturn, "customers received personal attention usually found only in luxury showrooms . . . As a matter of policy, employees would drop what they were doing and cheer in the showroom when a customer received the keys to a new Saturn."[2] Launched with much fanfare, Saturn looked to be GM's silver bullet—the innovative strategic initiative that would finally turn things around.

As it turns out, Saturn did not turn things around. Some twenty years and, by analyst estimates, $20 billion in losses later, Saturn is gone. The division was shuttered and all of its dealerships closed by the end of 2010. GM, emerging from Chapter 11 bankruptcy, is now a shadow of its former self, and its US market share is less than 20 percent.[3] Launching Saturn didn't cause GM's bankruptcy, but it didn't help much, either. Saturn vehicles, though they garnered loyalty from owners, never reached the critical mass needed to sustain a full lineup of cars or a national dealer network. As one former GM director said of Saturn, "it may well be the biggest fiasco in automotive history since Ford brought out the Edsel."[4]

The folks running Saturn aspired to participate in the US small-car segment with younger buyers. By contrast, Toyota, Honda, and Nissan all aspired to win in that segment. Guess what happened? Toyota, Honda, and Nissan all aimed for the top, making the hard strategic choices and substantial investments required to win. GM, through Saturn, aimed to play and invested to that much lower standard. Initially Saturn did OK as a brand. But it needed substantial resources to keep up against Toyota, Honda, and Nissan, all of which were investing at breakneck speed. GM couldn't and wouldn't keep up. Saturn died, not because it made bad cars, but because its aspirations were simply too modest to keep it alive. The aspirations did not spur winning where-to-play and how-to-win choices, capabilities, and management systems.

To be fair, GM had myriad challenges that made playing to win a daunting prospect—troubling union relations, oppressive legacy health-care and pension costs, and difficult dealer regulations. However, playing to play, rather than seeking to play to win, perpetuated the overall corporate problems rather than overcoming them. Contrast the approach at GM to the approach at P&G, where the company plays to win whenever it chooses to play. And the approach holds even in the unlikeliest of places. Playing to win is reasonably straightforward to contemplate in a consumer market. But what does it look like for an internal, shared-services function? Even there, you can play to win, as Filippo Passerini, president of P&G's global business services (GBS) unit demonstrates.

Playing to Win

At the end of the dot-com bubble, the IT world was in turmoil. The NASDAQ had melted down, taking both the credibility of the high-tech industry and the broader market indexes with it, throwing the economy into a recession. Yet, despite the crash, it was clear that spending on IT infrastructure and services would continue to increase. IT services were far from a core competency for most companies (including P&G), and the costs and complexities of providing IT services in-house were daunting. Fortunately, riding to the rescue was a new breed of service provider: the business process outsourcer (BPO). These companies (including IBM, EDS, Accenture, TCS, and Infosys) would provide a range of IT services from the outside, managing complexity for a fee. As the postcrash dust cleared, rapidly digitizing companies were faced with decisions on how much to use BPOs, which BPO partner to select, and how best to do so. It wasn't easy; the implications of a poor choice could be millions of dollars in extra costs and untold headaches down the line.

At P&G, many of the operations that might be outsourced had been gathered together in a 1999 reorganization. This GBS function was responsible for business services including IT, facilities management, and employee services. In 2000, three options for the future of GBS were being actively explored: stay the course and continue to run GBS internally; spin off GBS (partly or wholly) to allow it to become a major player in the BPO business; or outsource most of GBS to one of the biggest existing BPO companies.

It was not an easy decision. The stock markets and economy were cratering, as were the stock prices of the publicly traded BPOs. If completed, the deal would have been highly complex and at an unprecedented size for the global BPO industry. P&G had never outsourced or sold anything affecting this many employees, so the impact on morale and culture was highly uncertain. As the options were made known to employees, some employees feared the company would sell loyal P&G employees into "slavery."

The easiest thing would have been to declare that the issue was too divisive and to stick with the status quo. After all, GBS was working just fine. It was playing well in its space and delivering high-quality services to a wide range of internal customers. Alternatively, P&G could have gone with the next most conventional option: a single large deal with a premier BPO firm like IBM Global Services or EDS. Finally, the company could have acknowledged that a large, in-house global services organization was an inefficient use of P&G resources and spun out GBS into its own BPO. Any of these choices might have seemed sensible given the circumstances. But none effectively answered the question of how P&G could win with its global services.

The senior team wasn't convinced that all of the options were on the table. So, Filippo Passerini, who had a strong IT background and marketing management experience, was asked to think through the existing options and, if appropriate, suggest additional possibilities. Passerini struggled with the conventional choice. In theory, outsourcing to a single large BPO would create considerable economies of scale. It was clear that the deal would be good for the BPO partner, which would secure the biggest outsourcing deal in the industry's history. But there was no obvious reason why the deal would help P&G to win. P&G wanted more than cost-effectiveness and a commitment to a predefined service level from an outsourcing deal. It wanted flexibility, a partner that could and would innovate with P&G to create value that didn't exist in the current structure.

Passerini soon came up with a new option. Instead of signing one deal, P&G would outsource various GBS activities to best-of-breed BPO partners, finding one ideal partner to manage facilities, another to manage IT infrastructure, and so on. The logic of this best-of-breed option was that P&G's needs are highly varied and that a variety of more specialized partners would be most capable of meeting the needs. Passerini saw that specialization could increase the quality and lower the cost of BPO solutions, and believed that P&G could manage the complexity of multiple relationships to create more value than it could through one relationship. Plus, there was risk mitigation in having multiple partners, and they could be benchmarked against one another to promote better performance. Finally, outsourcing would free up remaining GBS resources to invest in P&G core capabilities and build sustainable competitive advantage.

The case for a best-of-breed approach was compelling. In 2003, P&G entered BPO partnerships with Hewlett-Packard in IT support and applications, IBM Global Services in employee services, and Jones Lang Lasalle in facilities management. Importantly, Passerini didn't simply select the biggest or best-known player in each BPO space. In fact, as he explains, he chose partners considering another essential criterion: "For each one of them, there was a common denominator: interdependency. It played out in different ways. For HP, they were a distant fourth player in the industry. With P&G, they gained instantaneous visibility and credibility. As important as they are to us, because all of our systems operate on the HP platform now, we are equally important to them [as their lead customer]. For each one of the [best-in-breed partners], the benefit was different, but each one of them became interdependent with P&G."[5] Passerini had crafted a richer way of thinking about the BPO relationship, one that asked, under what conditions can we help each other win?

Passerini's approach has been a success. The three original partnerships have performed well and have led to a handful of deeper partnerships for different services. The cost of services has fallen. Meanwhile, quality has risen and service levels have improved. Satisfaction rates for the six thousand employees who transferred to the BPO partners went up too; they are now a core part of their new organizations rather than a noncore part of P&G. And the approach has freed up P&G's GBS team members to focus on innovating and building IT systems that support P&G strategic choices and capabilities, like designing state-of-the-art virtual shopping experiences for consumer insights work and a desktop-based "cockpit" that provides P&G leaders with at-a-glance decision-making tools. GBS has been able to outsource the utilities element of P&G's shared services and focus internally on areas where it can build strategic advantage. P&G's approach to this set of transactions has become a model for other organizations, as multiple rather than single-source BPOs are becoming a preferred industry norm.

If the aspiration for GBS was to come to a good-enough solution, then the best-of-breed option would never have been created. But the aspiration was considerably higher. The questions asked were these: What choice would help P&G win? And how could that choice create sustainable competitive advantage? These questions continue to be asked. Now head of a more agile GBS organization, Passerini thinks about providing service to P&G in terms of creating a winning value equation. "I fear becoming a commodity," he says. "[In IT] you need to be distinctive to avoid commoditization. We have been on a quest to deliver unique value to P&G. Whatever is distinctive and unique, we focus on; whatever is commodity, because there is not competitive advantage in doing it inside, we outsource."

The desire to win spurs a helpfully competitive mind-set, a desire to do better whenever possible. For this reason, GBS competes for its internal customers. Passerini explains: "We don't mandate new services; we offer them [to businesses and functions] at a cost. If the business units like them, they will buy them. If they don't like them, they will pass." This open market provides important feedback and keeps GBS thinking about how to win with its internal customers and create new value. So much so that Passerini famously stood at a global leadership team meeting and promised: "Give me anything I can turn into a service, and I'll save you seventeen cents on the dollar." It was a provocative offer, and one that set the tone for his team. Good enough wasn't an option. Providing services wasn't the strategy. Providing better services at higher quality and lower costs—while serving as an innovation engine for the company—was the strategy. It was a strategy aimed at winning.

With Those Who Matter Most

To set aspirations properly, it is important to understand who you are winning with and against. It is therefore important to be thoughtful about the business you're in, your customers, and your competitors. We asked P&G's businesses to focus on winning with those who matter most and against the very best. We wanted them to focus outward on their most important consumers and very best competitors, rather than inward on their own products and innovations.

Most companies, if you ask them what business they're in, will tell you what their product line is or will detail their service offering. Many handheld phone manufacturers, for example, would say they are in the business of making smartphones. They would not likely say that they are in the business of connecting people and enabling communication any place, any time. But that is the business they are actually in—and a smartphone is just one way to accomplish that. Or think of a skin-care company. It is far more likely to say it makes a line of skin-care products than to say it is in the business of helping women have healthier, younger-looking skin or helping women feel beautiful. It's a subtle difference, but an important one.

The former descriptions are examples of marketing myopia, something economist Theodore Levitt identified a half-century ago and a danger that is alive and well today. Companies in the grips of marketing myopia are blinded by the products they make and are unable to see the larger purpose or true market dynamics. These companies spend billions of dollars making their new generation of products just slightly better than their old generation of products. They use entirely internal measures of progress and success—patents, technical achievements, and the like—without stepping back to consider the needs of consumers and the changing marketplace or asking what business they are really in, which consumer need they answer, and how best to meet that need.

The biggest danger of having a product lens is that it focuses you on the wrong things—on materials, engineering, and chemistry. It takes you away from the consumer. Winning aspirations should be crafted with the consumer explicitly in mind. The most powerful aspirations will always have the consumer, rather than the product, at the heart of them. In P&G's home-care business, for instance, the aspiration is not to have the most powerful cleanser or most effective bleach. It is to reinvent cleaning experiences, taking the hard work out of household chores. It is an aspiration that leads to market-shifting products like Swiffer, the Mr. Clean Magic Eraser, and Febreze.

Against the Very Best

Then there is competition. When setting winning aspirations, you must look at all competitors and not just at those you know best. Of course, start with the usual suspects. Look at your biggest competitors, your historical competitors—for P&G, they are Unilever, Kimberly-Clark, and Colgate-Palmolive. But then expand your thinking to focus on the best competitor in your space, looking far and wide to determine just who that competitor might be.

This was the approach that we sought to foster at P&G. In different industries and categories, the best competitors were often found to be local companies, private-label competitors, and smaller consumer-goods companies. In this way, the home-care team came to focus on Reckitt-Benckiser (makers of Calgon, Woolite, Lysol, and Air Wick).

It wasn't easy to convince the team leaders to take Reckitt-Benckiser more seriously. But looking at the Reckitt-Benckiser competitive position versus P&G's—the competitor's performance results versus P&G's—was illustrative. P&G had a run of six years of strong revenue and double-digit earnings per share growth, and Reckitt-Benckiser was outperforming even that. It wasn't so much about Reckitt-Benckiser itself as it was about getting the general managers to question their assumptions and their current judgments. The push was to ask, "Who really is your best competitor?

More importantly, what are they doing strategically and operationally that is better than you? Where and how do they outperform you? What could you learn from them and do differently?" Looking at the best competitor, no matter which company it might be, provides helpful insights into the multiple ways to win.

Summing Up

The essence of great strategy is making choices—clear, tough choices, like what businesses to be in and which not to be in, where to play in the businesses you choose, how you will win where you play, what capabilities and competencies you will turn into core strengths, and how your internal systems will turn those choices and capabilities into consistently excellent performance in the marketplace. And it all starts with an aspiration to win and a definition of what winning looks like.

Unless winning is the ultimate aspiration, a firm is unlikely to invest the right resources in sufficient amounts to create sustainable advantage. But aspirations alone are not enough. Leaf through a corporate annual report, and you will almost certainly find an aspirational vision or mission statement. Yet, with most corporations, it is very difficult to see how the mission statement translates into real strategy and ultimately strategic action. Too many top managers believe their strategy job is largely done when they share their aspiration with employees. Unfortunately, nothing happens after that. Without explicit where-to-play and how-to-win choices connected to the aspiration, a vision is frustrating and ultimately unfulfilling for employees. The company needs where and how choices in order to act. Without them, it can't win. The next chapter will turn to the question of where to play.

WINNING ASPIRATION DOS AND DON'TS

✓ Do play to win, rather than simply to compete. Define winning in your context, painting a picture of a brilliant, successful future for the organization.

✓ Do craft aspirations that will be meaningful and powerful to your employees and to your consumers; it isn't about finding the perfect language or the consensus view, but is about connecting to a deeper idea of what the organization exists to do.

✓ Do start with consumers, rather than products, when thinking about what it means to win.

✓ Do set winning aspirations (and make the other four choices) for internal functions and outward-facing brands and business lines. Ask, what is winning for this function? Who are its customers, and what does it mean to win with them?

✓ Do think about winning relative to competition. Think about your traditional competitors, and look for unexpected "best" competitors too.

✓ Don't stop here. Aspirations aren't strategy; they are merely the first box in the choice cascade.

STRATEGY AS WINNING

A.G. Lafley

In my now forty-plus years in business, I have found that most leaders do not like to make choices. They'd rather keep their options open. Choices force their hands, pin them down, and generate an uncomfortable degree of personal risk. I've also found that few leaders can truly define winning. They generally speak of short-term financial measures or a simple share of a narrowly defined market. In effect, by thinking about options instead of choices and failing to define winning robustly, these leaders choose to play but not to win. They wind up settling for average industry results at best.

The P&G I joined in the late 1970s was not very good at making choices and defining winning. In June 1977, I reported for duty as a brand assistant in the US laundry division, affectionately known as Big Soap. At the time, P&G sold fifteen laundry detergent and laundry soap brands and five dish detergent brands, considerably more than consumers needed or wanted, and more than its retail customers could profitably distribute, merchandise, and sell. Today, P&G has five laundry and three dish brands. Meanwhile, the business has consistently grown its net sales, market share, gross and operating margin, and value creation. Most importantly, P&G became the clear-cut leader in the US market. Once-formidable competitors Colgate-Palmolive and Unilever have effectively exited the categories in the United States; they've turned their remaining brands into contract-manufactured store brands, which in most cases are a weak third player to P&G and private-label brands. P&G's victory in the North American laundry category is the culmination of a series of clear, connected, and mutually reinforcing strategic choices that began to be made in the early 1980s. A series of sector, category, and brand leaders have committed to winning in this category and have successfully found ways to do so.

Even as P&G got better at defining winning at the brand and category level, it hasn't always had the same clarity at the company level, which has resulted in periods of underperformance. In the early 1980s, company leadership was frustrated by slowing top-line volume and sales growth rates and gave the direction to stimulate top-line growth organically and through acquisition. Without a clear strategy as to where to play or how to win, the result was a mishmash of acquisitions that never returned the cost of capital (Orange Crush, Ben Hill Griffin, Bain de Soleil, et al.) and a raft of failed new brands and new products, including Abound, Citrus Hill, Cold Snap, Encaprin, Solo, and Vibrant. In 1984–1985, the company experienced its first down profit year since World War II. In 1986, it took its first major restructuring and write-off. At that point, the call went out to Michel Porter and Monitor. It was P&G's first experience with business strategy, and I was fortunate to be one of the guinea pigs in Porter's first class.

Unfortunately, the first inoculation didn't take. When the business began to get better, thanks to another major restructuring and stronger international growth, and the short-term financial results began to improve, P&G forgot most of what it had learned. When top-line growth slowed again in the late 1990s, the company reverted to the same helter-skelter, new-categories and new-brands, and M&A approach. This time, the bets were even bigger on new products and new technologies, including robots to clean homes, paper cups and plates, even new retail formats. And acquisitions ranged more broadly, including the PUR water company and the Iams pet food company. P&G seriously looked at Eastman Kodak Company, lost an auction to Pfizer for American Home Products, and pursued Warner-Lambert in an attempt to buy its way into the pharmaceuticals business. Not surprisingly, the wheels came off again.

By the time of my election to CEO in 2000, most of P&G's businesses were missing their goals, many by a wide margin. The company was overinvested and overextended. It was not winning with those who mattered most—consumers and customers. When I visited all our top retailers in my first thirty days on the job, I found that P&G was their biggest supplier but nowhere near their best supplier. Consumers were abandoning P&G, as evidenced by declining trial rates and market share on most of our leading brands.

I was determined to get P&G's strategy right. To me, *right* meant that P&G would focus on achievable ways to win with the consumers who mattered the most and against the very best competition. It meant leaders would make real strategic choices (identifying what they would do and not do, where they would play and not play, and how specifically they would create competitive advantage to win). And it meant that leaders at all levels of the company would become capable strategists as well as capable operators. I was going to teach strategy until P&G was excellent at it.

I wanted my team to understand that strategy is disciplined thinking that requires tough choices and is all about winning. Grow or grow faster is not a strategy. Build market share is not a strategy. Ten percent or greater earnings-per-share growth is not a strategy. Beat XYZ competitor is not a strategy. A strategy is a coordinated and integrated set of where-to-play, how-to-win, core capability, and management system choices that uniquely meet a consumer's needs, thereby creating competitive advantage and superior value for a business. Strategy is a way to win—and nothing less.

Chapter Three

Where to Play

For decades, Bounty was a stalwart brand for P&G. From the 1970s to the 1990s, television commercials featuring Nancy Walker as a diner waitress (and paper towel aficionado) named Rosie established the paper towel brand in the hearts and minds of consumers. The ads' tagline—"The quicker picker-upper"—was as well known as American Express's "Don't leave home without it" or Maxwell House's "Good to the last drop." A proprietary technology advantage meant that Bounty really was more absorbent than competitive brands, and it became the leading paper towel brand in North America. Even after Rosie retired, the brand continued to grow, adding a share point per year, like clockwork.

But by the late 1990s, the Bounty business was struggling. North America had always been Bounty's best and biggest market, but as P&G focused on a globalization agenda, the tissue and towel team (which was responsible for Bounty, Charmin toilet paper, and Puffs facial tissues) had embarked on a global buying spree, acquiring brands and manufacturing capacity in Europe, Asia, and Latin America. The acquisitions consumed cash and constrained growth and profitability in the core US market. By the time Charlie Pierce came on as president of global family care (the renamed tissue and towel business) in 2001, it was time to change course. As Pierce puts it, "I think my job was to declare crisis."[1]

The global expansion was clearly problematic, but so too was the lack of strategic focus, particularly in R&D. The family-care team, inspired by corporate stretch goals to think big, was working on tangential, white-space ideas, like plastic-wrap technology, food containers, and paper plates. These new products might turn out to be worthy initiatives, but they had little connection to better paper towels, toilet paper, and facial tissue. Some of the team had come to believe that global family care could never get great financial returns from the structurally unattractive tissue and towel business, so it looked to other products and segments for growth. Pierce recalls his initial reaction: "If it is true that we can't get a decent return from the existing business, we should get out of the business entirely."

Was it true? P&G had made corporate where-to-play choices to grow in and from the core; to extend into home-care, beauty, health, and personal-care categories; and to build presence in emerging markets. Across these choices, P&G believed it could win through its ability to understand core consumers, by creating and building differentiated brands, and through R&D, innovative product design, global scale, and strong partnerships with both suppliers and channel customers. All of this presented a challenge for family care. In Europe, Asia, and Latin America, manufacturing overcapacity and private-label dominance were turning the category into a commodity. In emerging markets, prices and willingness to pay were so low that brand differentiation conferred little to no advantage. A niche strategy in emerging markets—to target just those few customers who valued premium performance—was nearly impossible because the capital requirements to make paper products mean a business must have substantial scale to be economical. Yet, the idea of building a truly global tissue and towel business was untenable.

The good news was that the business could be structurally attractive in North America; P&G could have a billion-dollar leadership brand with significant manufacturing economies of scale from North American sales alone. The family-care team could pare back and choose to play only in North America, in the top half of the market and, over time, sell off its assets in the rest of the world. Paring back was a choice P&G had made before. The company had chosen to enter or stay in categories that were generally unattractive structurally, but it had played in only the potentially attractive segments, working hard on pricing, capital and operating expenses, product and package design, operating costs, and scale. Laundry care, feminine care, and fine fragrances had all been written off as unwinnable categories, before P&G found a way to play to its strengths in only the most attractive segments. In each case, choosing where to play explicitly involved choosing where not to play as well, all within an overall industry structure.

With geography decided, where-to-play shifted to products. When the where-to-play choice was a global one, the innovation team had logically decided to pursue a series of new products and categories, like food containers and paper cups, that were outside the core of paper towels and tissues. Given the unattractive nature of the global tissue and towel businesses, it made some sense to test potentially more profitable product categories. But this approach meant that instead of innovating on its existing products, the team was chasing more-speculative product categories. Once the geographic choice was narrowed, family care could reorient the product where-to-play choice back to the core business, focusing on improving its competitive position in paper towels and bath and facial tissue. It could focus on Bounty, Charmin, and Puffs again.

The team began with Bounty and with consumers. Deep consumer understanding is at the heart of the strategy discussion. To be effective, strategy must be rooted in a desire to meet user needs in a way that creates value for both the company and the consumer. In considering where to play among consumer segments, the Bounty team asked some critical questions: Who is the consumer? What is the job to be done? Why do consumers choose what they do, relative to the job to be done? Bounty had tremendous awareness and brand equity in the North American marketplace. "It had by far the best equity in its category—one of the strongest brand equities in the company," says Pierce. "If you asked, virtually 100 percent of people would say Bounty is a great brand and a really good product. Then some would go off and buy something else. What's wrong with this picture?" Pierce and his team set out to truly understand consumer needs, habits, and practices as they relate to paper towels.

In watching and talking to consumers, they found that there were three distinct types of paper towel users. The first group cared about both strength and absorbency. For this group, Bounty was a perfect fit—a great combination of the two attributes they cared most about. The team found that among these consumers, Bounty was already the clear winner. Here, "Bounty didn't have a forty share," Pierce says. "It had an eighty share."

But many consumers didn't fit into the strength-and-absorbency category; those consumers fell squarely into the remaining two segments. The second segment consisted of consumers who wanted a paper towel with a cloth-like feel. They didn't care much about strength or absorbency, certainly much less than the core Bounty group did. Rather, this group of customers cared about how soft the paper towel felt in their hand. The final segment had price as their top priority, though not as their sole concern, says Pierce: "The need of those consumers was also on strength. It wasn't at all on absorbency, because they had a compensating behavior to address the absorbency shortfalls of lower-priced paper-towel products: they would simply use more sheets." These consumers were happy to use more sheets of a lower-priced paper towel, when needed, rather than spend more money for a premium brand that enabled the use of fewer sheets each time. It was a trade-off that made good sense to them.

Bounty had captured most of the first consumer segment, but had made few inroads with the other two groups. Pierce wanted to play in all three segments to achieve more scale and enhance profitability. Going forward, Bounty would become not one but three distinct products—each one designed to target a specific consumer segment. Traditional Bounty would remain unchanged and serve the first segment, which already loved the brand. A new product called Bounty Extra Soft would target the consumers who craved a soft, cloth-like feel. And then there was the final segment—the strength-and-price segment. These consumers presented something of a challenge.

Most of the lower-priced paper towels on the market were of poor quality, and the Bounty team didn't want to devalue the core brand by associating it with a subpar product. "Those products fail miserably on strength," Pierce notes. "They shred, they tear. They disintegrate in the face of a spill. Then, you not only have to deal with the spill, but you also have the mess of the towel residue to deal with." To have the Bounty name—even at a value price point—a product would have to live up to the equity of the Bounty brand. The new offering for the strength-and-price segment was designed not as a stripped-down version of Bounty, but as a new product with specific consumer needs in mind. Bounty Basic was considerably stronger than any other value brand and priced at about 75 percent of the cost of regular Bounty. Shelved away from traditional Bounty, with the other lower-priced brands, it spoke directly to the third segment of consumers.

While there was some concern that existing Bounty consumers might trade down to Bounty Basic, the relative attributes of the three products fit each segment's needs so perfectly that little shifting actually occurred. Pierce notes, "The old Bounty was one product that existed for decades. The modern-day Bounty is now three products that were designed against very clear consumer understanding and consumer segmentation. They're all very different from each other on a product performance standpoint, and each is designed to meet the needs of its users."

Ultimately, the family-care team chose not to play in the truly commodity portion of the market; while Bounty Basic is a value offering, it is priced at a premium to private-label brands and offers a clear strength advantage. By staying in the noncommodity space, in terms of both product assortment and price point, P&G can target its core consumers through its most valued core retailers (its best and biggest customers), levering core advantages in innovation and brand building. Pierce and his team made where-to-play choices on geography (North America), consumers (three segments in the top half of the market), products (paper towels, branded basic and premium), channels (grocery stores, mass discounters, drugstores, and membership club stores like Costco), and stages of production (R&D and production of the paper towel itself, but not growing, harvesting, or pulping the trees). Making these clear where-to-play choices, for Bounty and the family-care category, spurred innovation and helped powerful brands grow even stronger. As a result, P&G family care consistently delivered business growth and value creation at industry-leading levels.

The Importance of the Right Playing Field

The choice of where to play defines the playing field for the company (or brand, or category, etc.). It is a question of what business you are really in. It is a choice about where to compete and where not to compete. Understanding this choice is crucial, because the playing field you choose is also the place where you will need to find ways to win. Where-to-play choices occur across a number of domains, notably these:

- *Geography.* In what countries or regions will you seek to compete?

- *Product type.* What kinds of products and services will you offer?

- *Consumer segment.* What groups of consumers will you target? In which price tier? Meeting which consumer needs?

- *Distribution channel.* How will you reach your customers? What channels will you use?

- *Vertical stage of production.* In what stages of production will you engage? Where along the value chain? How broadly or narrowly?

Many individual considerations need to go into the comprehensive where-to-play choice. And the considerations are the same, no matter the size of the company or type of industry. Think of a small farmer. He must answer a number of questions to get a clear sense of his playing field. Will he sell only locally or to his friends and neighbors, or will he attempt to join a co-op that has a larger geographic footprint? Which fruits and vegetables will he grow? Will he sell organic products or standard ones? Will he sell bushels of fruit unprocessed or process apples into juice before selling them? Will he sell direct to consumers, or through a warehouse middleman? If he does process the fruit into juice, will he do that himself or outsource that phase of production? If he is thoughtful, the farmer will consider where to play in a manner that enables him to choose geographies, segments, products, channels, and production options that work well together (e.g., selling organic veggies locally at farmer's markets or processing fruit to sell nationally while minimizing spoilage).

Start-ups, small businesses, regional or national companies, and even huge multinationals all face an analogous set of where-to-play choices. The answers, of course, differ. Small businesses may well have narrower where-to-play choices than larger companies do, largely as a function of capacity and scale. But even the largest companies must make explicit choices to compete in some places, with some products, for some customers (and not in others). A choice to serve everyone, everywhere—or to simply serve all comers—is a losing choice.

Choosing where to play is also about choosing where not to play. This is more straightforward when you are considering where to expand (or not), but considerably harder when considering if you should stay in the places and segments you currently serve. The status quo—continuing on in the locations and segments you've always been—is all too often an implicit, unexamined choice. Simply because you have made a given where-to-play choice in the past is not a reason to stay there. Consider a company like General Electric. A decade ago, it derived considerable revenue from its entertainment holdings (NBC and Universal) and materials businesses (plastic and silicon). Today, it has remade its portfolio to focus much more on infrastructure, energy, and transportation, where its distinctive capabilities can make a real difference to winning. This was an explicit choice about where not to play.

Inevitably, the significance of each dimension of the where-to-play choice will vary by context. Each dimension must be considered thoughtfully and will hold different weight in different situations. A start-up might focus first on the products or services to be offered. A stagnating giant might focus on customers—looking for a deeper understanding of needs and new ways to approach segmentation—to narrow and refine an overly broad where-to-play choice.

At P&G, where to play choices start with the consumer: Who is she? What does the consumer want and need? To win with mom, P&G invests heavily in truly understanding her—through observation, through home visits, through a significant investment in uncovering unmet and unexpressed needs. Only through a concerted effort to understand the consumer, her needs, and the way in which P&G can best serve those needs is it possible to effectively determine where to play—which businesses to enter or leave, which products to sell, which markets to prioritize, and so on. As current CEO Bob McDonald explains, "We don't give lip service to consumer understanding. We dig deep. We immerse ourselves in people's day-to-day lives. We work hard to find the tensions that we can help resolve. From those tensions come insights that lead to big ideas."[2] Those big ideas can be the basis of a powerful where-to-play choice.

The distribution channel choice also tends to loom large for P&G, because of the dominant size and market power of the retailers in question. Tesco has more than 30 percent of the UK market.[3] Walmart serves some 200 million Americans every week.[4] Other players, like Loblaw in Canada or Carrefour in Europe, have substantial regional presence. For this reason, channel is a particularly crucial where-to-play consideration for the company. Of course, for some industries, there is no real channel consideration (e.g., in service industries that deal directly with the end consumer). Again, context matters—and each company must assess the weight of the different where-to-play choices for itself.

One final consideration for where to play is the competitive set. Just as it does when it defines winning aspirations, a company should make its where-to-play choices with the competition firmly in mind. Choosing a playing field identical to a strong competitor's can be a less attractive proposition than tacking away to compete in a different way, for different customers, or in different product lines. But strategy isn't simply a matter of finding a distinctive path. A company may choose to play in a crowded field or in one with a dominant competitor if the company can bring new and distinctive value. In such a case, winning may mean targeting the lead competitor right away or going after weaker competitors first.

So it was with Tide. When Liquid Tide was introduced in 1984, P&G was entering the liquid-detergent category against a strong, established competitor. Even with strong brand equity from its powdered detergent, this wouldn't be an easy win. Wisk, Unilever's market-leading liquid detergent, was a powerful, established brand with loyal customers. For the first two or three years, Wisk did not give up a share point against Liquid Tide. In Liquid Tide's first year, Wisk actually gained share. Clearly, Wisk users weren't moving to Tide. But P&G didn't need to steal Wisk users to win in the category, at least not right away. The high-profile launch of Liquid Tide helped expand the overall liquid-detergent category, and P&G picked up the lion's share of the expansion. Liquid Tide created new consumers for liquid detergent, and none of them had a loyalty to Wisk. As the category grew, Tide could begin to take share from smaller players, like Dynamo, which couldn't compete with P&G's R&D, scale, and brand-building expertise. Only then, having built critical mass, would Liquid Tide need to go after Wisk directly. At that point, the battle was all but won.

For Liquid Tide, it wasn't a matter of avoiding a playing field that held a fierce competitor. It was about expanding the playing field to make room for the two competitors and creating time to gain momentum. In the end, Liquid Tide won and took the market lead decisively.

Three Dangerous Temptations

As we've noted, there is a lot to consider when crafting a winning where-to-play choice, from consumers to channels and customers; to competition; to local, regional, and global differences. In the face of that kind of complexity, your strategy can easily fall prey to oversimplification, resignation, even desperation. In particular, you should avoid three pitfalls when thinking about where to play. The first is to refuse to choose, attempting to play in every field all at once. The second is to attempt to buy your way out of an inherited and unattractive choice. The third is to accept a current choice as inevitable or unchangeable. Giving in to any one of these temptations leads to weak strategic choices and, often, to failure.

Failing to Choose

Focus is a crucial winning attribute. Attempting to be all things to all customers tends to result in underserving everyone. Even the strongest company or brand will be positioned to serve some customers better than others. If your customer segment is "everyone" or your geographic choice is "everywhere," you haven't truly come to grips with the need to choose. But, you may argue, don't companies like Apple and Toyota choose to serve everyone? No, not really. While they do have very large customer bases, the companies don't serve all parts of the world and all customer segments equally. As late as 2009, Apple derived just 2 percent of its revenue from China. That was a choice—about where and when to play.

It was a choice based on resources, capabilities, and an understanding that even Apple can't be everywhere at once.

P&G, too, can't serve all markets equally well. With Bounty, it chose to target three segments of consumers in the top end of the North American paper towel market; it chose not to serve the rest of the world or consumers for whom price was the primary decision criteria. For P&G overall, in choosing where to play in emerging markets, the focus was on regions where it had an established business (like Mexico) and where new markets opened equally to all comers at the same time (e.g., Eastern Europe right after the fall of the Berlin Wall and China when Deng Xiaoping opened the first enterprise zones in Guangzhou City). The decision to focus on a very few emerging markets at a time enabled P&G to prioritize resource allocation, cash, and, most importantly, people, against moving up the learning curve and establishing successful businesses. Without such an explicit choice, P&G would have wound up with a mix of middling businesses scattered around the world, all starved for the attention and resources needed to become a market leader.

Trying to Buy Your Way Out of an Unattractive Game

Companies often attempt to move out of an unattractive game and into an attractive one through acquisition. Unfortunately, it rarely works. A company that is unable to strategize its way out of a current challenging game will not necessarily excel at a different one—not without a thoughtful approach to building a strategy in both industries. Most often, an acquisition adds complexity to an already scattered and fragmented strategy, making it even harder to win overall.

Resource companies are particularly susceptible to this trap, as they often lust after the value-added producers in their industries. Whether in aluminum, newsprint, or coal, an acquirer is often seduced by the idea of access to the higher prices and faster growth rates of a downstream industry. Unfortunately, there are two big problems with this kind of acquisition. The first is price. It costs a great deal to buy into attractive industries—quite often, acquirers must pay more than the asset could ever be worth to them, which dooms the acquirer in the long run. Second, the strategy and capabilities required in the targeted industry are often very different from those in the current industry; it is seriously tough sledding to bridge the two approaches and have an advantage in both (in mining bauxite and processing aluminum, for instance). Such acquisitions tend to be both overly expensive and strategically challenging.

Rather than attempting to acquire your way into a more attractive position, you can set a better goal for your company. The real goal should be to create an internal discipline of strategic thinking that enables a more thoughtful approach to the current game, regardless of industry, and connects to possible different futures and opportunities.

Accepting an Existing Choice as Immutable

It can also be tempting to view a where-to-play choice as a given, as having been made for you. But a company always has a choice of where to play. To return to a favorite example, Apple wasn't bound entirely by its first where-to-play choice—which was desktop computers. Though it eventually established a comfortable niche in that world, as the desktop of choice for creative industries, Apple chose to change its playing field to move into the portable communication and entertainment space with the iPod, iTunes, iPhone, and iPad.

It is tempting to think that you have no choice in where to play, because it makes for a great excuse for mediocre performance. It is not easy to change playing fields, but it is doable and can make all the difference. Sometimes the change is subtle, like a shift in consumer focus within a current industry—as with Olay. Other times the change can be dramatic, like at Thomson Corporation. Twenty years ago, the company's where-to-play choice was North American newspapers, North Sea oil, and European travel; today (as Thomson Reuters), it competes only in must-have, software-enhanced, subscription-based information delivered over the web. There is almost zero overlap between the old and new where-to-play choices for Thomson. The change didn't happen overnight—it took twenty years of dedicated work—but it demonstrates that changing an existing where-to-play choice is doable.

Even well-established brands have multiple choices. We've already seen the Olay where-to-play choice and how it changed over time. Rather than attempting to deliver products to all women, in all age categories, at the lower end of the market, the Olay team chose to compete primarily on a narrower field—women aged thirty-five-plus who were newly concerned with the signs of aging. This was just one of many possible choices for the brand, an explicit narrowing and shifting of the previous where-to-play choice. Then there is one of P&G's biggest brands: Tide. It gained strength by broadening its where-to-play choice.

Once, the Tide team was focused almost entirely on the dirt you can actually see on clothes. As late as the 1980s, Tide had two forms—the traditional washing powder and the liquid version—both geared at getting the visible dirt out of your clothes ("Tide's in, Dirt's out"). P&G broadened its where-to-play choice for Tide by moving beyond visible dirt. Tide introduced product versions designed to address a whole range of cleaning needs—Tide with Bleach, Tide Plus a Touch of Downy, Tide Plus Febreze, Tide for Coldwater, Tide Unscented; then, P&G expanded the Tide offering from detergents to other laundry-related products—creating a line of stain-release products, most notably the highly successful Tide-to-Go instant stain remover. The goal was to build a product line that effectively addressed different loads, different consumers, even different family members.

Tide expanded its distribution model as well. The team started to look at the distributors that offer a very limited number of brands, like drugstores, wholesale stores like Costco, dollar stores, and vending machines at self-service laundries and campgrounds. These channels tend to offer just one national brand and a private-label option. P&G pushed hard to have Tide chosen as the national brand in each case. As the leading brand in the category, it had a compelling case. The horizon has even expanded to Tide-branded dry cleaners. A broader definition of where to play served as the building block to extend the brand. Each new Tide product is built on the superior cleaning ability of Tide and its value-added benefits, reinforcing the core brand. In this way, Tide broadened to get stronger.

Imagining a New Where to Play

Sometimes the key to finding a new place to play is to simply believe that one is possible. In 1995, Chip Bergh was appointed general manager for P&G's US hard-surface cleaners business. Bergh reflects, with a laugh, "It sounds like a very nonelegant, unsexy business, and that's exactly what it was. It was not a strategic priority in the company. But interestingly, for all of our competitors, it was a core business. We knew our CEO never rolled out of bed and thought about this business. But for our competitors, every morning when the CEO was getting out of bed, he was worrying about this business."[5] The competitive landscape was challenging. Bergh's brands included past-their-prime names like Comet, Spic 'n Span, and Mr. Clean. It was, Bergh notes, "about a $200 million business at the time, and it was in free fall." At one point in the mid-1970s, Comet had enjoyed a 50 percent market share of the category. By 1995, all of P&G's brands in this category, combined, had less than 20 percent of the market.

Times had changed, and P&G had failed to change with them. There were fewer hard surfaces in homes, as fiberglass (and porous marbles and other stones) replaced porcelain. Competitors had introduced less abrasive cleansers that resonated with consumers; P&G had not. "It was clear we had to do something very, very different," Bergh notes. "We realized that our products were no longer relevant for the consumer and that we had been out-innovated."

So Bergh challenged his team to think about where to play from an entirely new perspective that would be grounded in an understanding of the competitive landscape and of P&G's core capabilities. "I took my leadership team off-site for two days," he says. "The focus was to come up with a set of choices that would make a difference on the business. The rallying cry we had around the new choices, and around the new strategy, was to fundamentally change the game of cleaning at home and make cleaning less of a chore." As ever, the starting point was consumer needs—like quick surface cleaning without muss and fuss, addressing a particular job and doing it better than current offerings. Bergh continues: "We asked, how do we leverage the company scale and size and technology expertise to fundamentally change cleaning at home? The key breakthrough for us was to start putting together different technologies that P&G had, but our competitors didn't. How do you marry chemistry, surfactant technology, and paper technology? All of that led, within two years, to the launch of Swiffer."

Swiffer proved to be a whole new where-to-play choice for the hard-surface cleaners business. It was a consumer-led blockbuster. *BusinessWeek* listed it as one of "20 Products That Shook the Stock Market."[6] Ten years later, Swiffer is now in 25 percent of US households. And as competition enters into the category it created, P&G is turning its attention to the next strategic frontier for Swiffer, asking what's next.

Digging Deeper

It can be easy to dismiss new and different where-to-play choices as risky, as a poor fit with the current business, or as misaligned with core capabilities. And it is just as easy to write off an entire industry on the basis of the predominant where-to-play choices made by the competitors in that industry. But sometimes, you must dig a bit deeper—to examine unexpected where-to-play choices from all sides—to truly understand what is possible and how an industry can be won with a new place to play. This was the case with fine fragrances at P&G.

The P&G fine-fragrance business had an inauspicious start. In fact, P&G's entry into the category was accidental. In 1991, the company acquired Max Factor to bolster the international reach of its color cosmetics business (entered in 1989 with the purchase of Noxell, the parent company that owned Cover Girl). Cover Girl was exclusively a North American brand at the time. Max Factor's cosmetics business was primarily outside North America and thus was a nice, logical fit. As it turned out, Max Factor had a tiny fragrance line—so now, P&G was in the fine-fragrance business too. In 1994, then chairman and CEO, Ed Artzt, acted to deepen P&G's participation in the fine-fragrance business with the purchase of Giorgio of Beverly Hills for $150 million. At the time, most thought it was a strange acquisition—staid, Midwestern P&G buying a chic Rodeo Drive perfumery.

In many ways, it was an odd mix. The fragrance business featured a combination of company-owned brands, like Giorgio, and external brands for which P&G licensed only the perfume rights, like Hugo Boss. For one of the world's acknowledged branding leaders, licensing presented a strange situation—having to depend entirely on another company to create an overall brand image, to which P&G would simply add a line of consistent fine-fragrance products. Very little of P&G's brand-building expertise appeared to come into play. Plus, the reputations of these fashion brands were highly volatile. They waxed and waned, and there seemed to be little that the brands could do (and even less that P&G could do) about it. Very, very few perfume brands endured and grew for decades, as Tide and Crest had done. Fragrances were also sold substantially through a channel in which P&G was otherwise not present—department stores and perfumeries. And finally, P&G's R&D labs couldn't easily develop streams of innovation of the sort that kept Bounty and Pantene ahead of their competitors. Fine fragrances felt more like the hope-in-a-bottle business: lots of hype and little real technology. The strategic choices and capabilities for fine fragrances had little in common with the choices for most other P&G businesses. No surprise, then, that the fragrance business struggled along during the 1990s, underperforming relative to the industry and to P&G's company standards.

On the surface at least, fine fragrances looked like an obvious choice for divestiture. The business appeared to have a tenuous fit with the broader P&G. What's more, it had these complicating features—fashion-house dependence and tricky distribution. P&G had no road map for running businesses like this internally, and there wasn't a good analog on the outside to benchmark against. P&G hadn't been in the portfolio for very long, especially in its post-Giorgio format, so there wasn't much of a track record either. The company came very close to divesting the business but instead reframed the thinking.

Fine fragrances, however, were important to hang on to, for two strategic reasons. First, a fine-fragrance presence was an important component of a credible and competitive beauty business. P&G wanted to be a beauty leader, on the strength of hair care (Pantene, Head & Shoulders) and skin care (Olay). But to be truly credible with the industry and consumers as a beauty player, the company needed a position in cosmetics and fragrances as well. The knowledge transfer between the different categories is significant, meaning that what you learn in cosmetics and fragrances—through both product R&D and consumer research—has a lot of spillover into hair care and skin care, and vice versa. In other words, just being in the fragrance business makes you better in beauty categories overall.

In addition, fragrance is a very important part of the hair-care experience—scent alone can significantly influence consumer product preferences. And it isn't just true in hair care, which leads to the second strategic reason to play in fine fragrances: in many household and other personal-care businesses, there were significant consumer segments that cared deeply about the sensory experience. P&G could affect consumer purchase intent with the right fragrance. It soon became clear that fragrance was an important part of creating delightful consumer experiences and that P&G was the biggest fragrance user in the world. This little fine-fragrance business was important well beyond its existing size; it was crucial to building core capabilities and systems that could differentiate and create competitive advantage for brands and products across the entire corporation.

So P&G not only held on to the fine-fragrances business, but also built it strategically. P&G turned the industry business model inside out by making a totally different set of strategic where-to-play and how-to-win choices. Within the fine-fragrances industry, there was a well-established way to do business: new fragrances were pushed out of the fashion studios and fragrance houses, down the fashion runway, and into department stores at Christmas time. Most new fragrance brands were launched for holiday shopping and began to decline by the next spring. It was a push-and-churn model. And in most cases, it was secondary to another, primary business: fashion.

By contrast, P&G started with the consumer, hiring its own internal team of master perfumers to design fragrances against specific consumer wants and needs, as well as brand concepts. It partnered with the very best fragrance-house perfumers and designers. Before long, P&G became the preferred innovation partner in the fine-fragrance space. P&G brands are consumer-centric, concept-led, and designed to delight consumers. As it dedicated time and attention to the fine-fragrance business, P&G attracted the best agency partners and won numerous awards for advertising, marketing, and packaging. It built product portfolios that expanded and strengthened its consumer user base. It built brands that became leaders in their segments.

Another norm for the fragrance industry was to compete most aggressively within the high-end women's market. Rather than go head-to-head with the biggest players, the P&G fine-fragrance team decided to attack along the line of least expectation and least resistance—in men's fragrances with Hugo Boss and in younger, sporty fragrances through a partnership with Lacoste. The competition was focused on women's classic and fashion fragrances, where existing sales and profits were. Choosing a different place to play gave the fine-fragrance team the time and opportunity to test its strategy and business model, to hone its capabilities, and to build confidence that it could win.

To win in fine fragrances, the team leveraged all it could from P&G's core capabilities. It used P&G brand-building expertise to assess the strength and value of brands to determine which fashion brands to license and how much to pay for them. It used an understanding of the discipline of strategy to match its choices with the choices of the licensors, creating greater value for both.

On the innovation front, world-leading expertise with scents enabled P&G to create licensed-brand products that were uniquely appealing to consumers and that could last beyond a season. And P&G's scale as the world's largest purchaser of fragrances enabled it to buy critical and expensive perfume ingredients at lower cost than any competitors could.

With all these capabilities applied full force to the business, P&G built a fragrance house with licenses from Dolce & Gabbana, Escada, Gucci, and others. In the process, P&G became one of the largest and most profitable fine-fragrance businesses in the world, less than two decades after a modest entry into the industry. Staying in the fine-fragrances business is a choice that seemed counterintuitive at first and required a new way of thinking about just where to play within it, but the choice has paid huge dividends to the company overall.

Some things, however, happen by way of serendipity, and the acquisition of Max Factor is a perfect case in point. Max Factor was acquired to make the P&G cosmetics business more global. That really never panned out. Max Factor did sufficiently poorly in North America that it was discontinued there. Nor did it provide much of a cosmetics platform outside North America. So, the acquisition would likely be called a failure, considering the intent of the purchase. But as it turns out, the cosmetics business came along with two businesses— a small fine-fragrances portfolio and a tiny, super-high-end Japanese skin-care business called SK-II. That fragrance portfolio became the seed of a multi-billion-dollar, world-leading fine-fragrances business. SK-II has expanded into international markets and has crossed the billion-dollar mark in global sales, with extremely attractive profitability. In this case, serendipity smiled on P&G—though it also took smart choices and hard work to realize the potential of the businesses.

The Heart of Strategy

Where to play is about understanding the possible playing fields and choosing between them. It is about selecting regions, customers, products, channels, and stages of production that fit well together—that are mutually reinforcing and that marry well with real consumer needs. Rather than attempt to serve everyone or simply buy a new playing field or accept your current choices as inevitable, find a strong set of where-to-play choices. Doing so requires deep understanding of users, the competitive landscape, and your own capabilities. It requires imagination and effort. And every so often, some luck doesn't hurt.

As you work through your own choices, recall that where-to-play choices are equally about where not to play. They take options off the table and create true focus for the organization. But there is no single right answer. For some companies or brands, a narrow choice works best. For others, a broader choice fits. Or it may be that the best option is a narrow customer choice within a broad geographic segment (or vice versa). As with all things, context matters.

The heart of strategy is the answer to two fundamental questions: where will you play, and how will you win there? The next chapter will turn to the second question and to the matter of creating integrated choices, in which where to play and how to win reinforce and support, rather than fight against, one another.

WHERE-TO-PLAY DOS AND DON'TS

✓ Do choose where you will play and where you will not play. Explicitly choose and prioritize choices across all relevant *where* dimensions (i.e., geographies, industry segments, consumers, customers, products, etc.).

✓ Do think long and hard before dismissing an entire industry as structurally unattractive; look for attractive segments
in which you can compete and win.

✓ Don't embark on a strategy without specific *where*
choices. If everything is a priority, nothing is. There is no
point in trying to capture all segments. You can't. Don't try.

✓ Do look for places to play that will enable you to attack
from unexpected directions, along the lines of least resistance. Don't attack walled cities or take on your strongest
competitors head-to-head if you can help it.

✓ Don't start wars on multiple fronts at once. Plan for your
competitors' reactions to your initial choices, and think
multiple steps ahead. No single choice needs to last forever, but it should last long enough to confer the advantage
you seek.

✓ Do be honest about the allure of white space. It is tempting to be the first mover into unoccupied white space.
Unfortunately, there is only one true first mover (as there
is only one low-cost player), and all too often, the imagined
white space is already occupied by a formidable competitor you just don't see or understand.

Chapter Four

How to Win

Ask Jeff Weedman, P&G's vice president of global business development, about the technology behind Glad ForceFlex trash bags, and it's clear he's an enthusiast. He pulls out a white Kitchen Catcher bag to demonstrate, opening the bag and holding it out to his guest.[1] "Take a look at that film," he says. "See those patterns in there? Those patterns allow us to put a lot more stretch into the material."[2] Weedman makes a fist and uses it to stretch a small section of the trash bag to its limit. It stretches past his elbow before it tears. "Because of P&G's expertise in diapers, we know an awful lot about how to manipulate film," he explains. "This uses less plastic than those thick bags, and it stretches significantly more." P&G-invented technology produces a plastic bag that is both strong and stretchable, but uses considerably less material. It means a better product for consumers, with greater capacity and less breakage, at a lower cost for the manufacturer.

Building on quilting technology developed for paper towels, the ForceFlex product marked a significant step forward in trash-bag technology. It came out of P&G labs along with a sister technology—a self-sealing plastic wrap. Imagine that you want to put a leftover piece of chicken into the freezer for consumption in a few days. You can wrap it in plastic wrap and hope that it doesn't get freezer burn through one of the many small gaps in the wrapping. Or, you can place it in an expensive (on a per-use basis) zip-top freezer bag. P&G scientists found an alternative option: take a relatively small piece of a new, technologically advanced plastic wrap from a package (similar to a Glad Wrap or Saran Wrap roll), put the chicken on top, fold the material over the chicken, press gently with your finger around the chicken, and—presto—you have a hermetically sealed pouch ready for the fridge or freezer.

The two new technologies were sufficiently exciting that P&G management agreed to test-market, starting with the sealing food wrap (branded Impress). It was arguably the less compelling of the two concepts: self-sealing plastic wrap offered a new benefit that might or might not be of interest to consumers, while an ultra-strong garbage bag solved a well-documented frustration for consumers (garbage bags that leak and tear). Nonetheless, Impress was the starting point.

Test-market consumers loved Impress. It shot to a more than 25 percent share almost immediately, at a 30 percent price premium over existing wraps. It clearly had unique product technology that the competition didn't have and that consumers valued. Now, normally at P&G, this kind of result leads to cheering, investment in a new brand, and a full national launch. But the team involved was cognizant of cautionary tales on this front and was reluctant to simply dive in with these new plastic technologies.

In the early 1980s, P&G scientists had developed a way to incorporate the daily recommended intake of calcium in a single serving of orange juice. And better yet, the calcium absorbed readily into the body instead of passing quickly through it, as was the case with existing calcium supplements. Plus, the calcium had no adverse impact on the taste of the orange juice. For all the women and children out there who had to drink milk just to get

their calcium, even if they were lactose intolerant or didn't actually enjoy guzzling milk, this was a big win. Like Impress decades
later, the new orange juice with calcium scored very well in consumer testing. It was launched nationally as Citrus Hill in 1983
against two formidable competitors—Minute Maid (a Coca-Cola
division) and the then-independent Tropicana (later acquired by
PepsiCo, Inc., to become yet another front in the Coke-Pepsi
war). The two competitors dominated the branded segment of
the market, with Tropicana staking out leadership in the fresh-
squeezed segment and Minute Maid in the bigger segment of
juice reconstituted from frozen concentrate. Citrus Hill would
compete with both.

Suffice it to say, Minute Maid and Tropicana fought their new
competitor as though their lives depended on it—which, given
P&G's reputation, was not likely an exaggeration. P&G always
aimed for leading market share in each category— and sometimes,
but rarely, settled for second place. So if P&G was allowed to succeed, the competitors saw, one of them would probably die and
both could be displaced. By all appearances, Minute Maid and
Tropicana treated the Citrus Hill launch as a battle for survival and
not just another competitive foray.

For P&G, this wasn't like entering a new category against hundreds of small cloth-diaper producers with the launch of Pampers,
or like mop manufacturers with Swiffer. Citrus Hill was going up
against two gigantic, deep-pocketed, and entrenched competitors.
Sadly for P&G, the orange juice wars turned out to be a humbling
experience. Citrus Hill never made meaningful headway against
the defenses of Minute Maid and Tropicana, and P&G exited the
business after a decade of frustration. The final insult was that the
brand had to be shuttered, rather than sold, because no one could
be found to buy it. The only bright spot was that P&G made a nice
annual profit post-exit, by licensing the calcium technology to its

two former competitors. It turned out that both firms were happy to pay to add an attractive benefit to their existing offerings.

Fast forward two decades: competitively, it was clear that Impress would be going up directly against The Clorox Company's leading Glad brand and SC Johnson's Saran Wrap; both were powerful brands with well-established product lines. Each came from one of P&G's biggest competitors in the home and cleaning products categories. The new trash bags would compete against leader Glad, plus the Reynolds Group Holdings' Hefty line. For P&G, going into business with these two technologies would mean again entering established markets against two great brand names, each backed by large, high-quality organizations. And as with Coke and Tropicana, Clorox, SC Johnson, and Reynolds would all be well aware of the dangers of giving P&G a foothold. They would all fight, and fight hard. Then there were the operational concerns. Launching Impress and the trash-bag technology would require huge capital investments in manufacturing infrastructure—expensive, industry-specific technology with which P&G had no experience.

In other words, as the team explored a possible new where-to-play choice, it struggled to find a truly compelling way to win on that playing field. Consumers loved the product. The technology was outstanding and proprietary. But technology and product alone wouldn't lead to victory—not in the face of tough competitive dynamics and high capital costs. Rather than simply launch the new technology and attempt to ride out the painful war that would ensue, we decided to explore entirely different approaches to winning in this space. In the past, if P&G couldn't use a technology, the company would license it to another company (as P&G had, for example, with the calcium additive after the decline of Citrus Hill). But given the size of the potential prize here, we wondered whether there wasn't something other than the extremes of launching and licensing. Jeff Weedman was tasked with finding a third way that would create more value for consumers and competitive advantage for P&G.

Weedman explored the possibilities. "We talked to competitors who were in the wrap space," he recalls. "We went out and said 'Do you want this technology?' We ran an auction." Multiple bids came in for the technology, in many different configurations. One of the most intriguing was from Clorox. Clorox had acquired the Glad brand of wraps and trash bags in 1999, when it purchased First Brands, outbidding P&G for the property at the time. As Larry Peiros, then group vice president at The Clorox Company (now executive vice president and chief operating officer) explains, "Glad was a challenging acquisition from the very beginning. Our products were pretty much undifferentiated, and raw material costs were escalating. Our biggest Glad business, trash bags, was threatened by an aggressive competitor in Hefty and parity-performing store brands. Our food-storage Glad products, Glad Cling Wrap and GladWare, were under pressure from Ziploc's leading food-storage business. The business was struggling, and it was clear we needed very major product development and capital investment to be successful over the long term."[3] But Clorox didn't have the kind of proprietary R&D expertise with materials and plastics that P&G did. Nor did it have P&G's massive scale. Plus, the Clorox team understood the implications if the P&G technology went to a rival company. So, the team came forward with an unusual pitch for a larger partnership.

"There were a lot of reasons why we wanted a deeper relationship than just licensing," Peiros recalls. "Procter is a technology machine. They compete in many multi-billion-dollar categories in which they are developing new innovations. Some of those innovations would be applicable to bags and wraps. If P&G was willing to give us access to both existing and future technology for our category, that could be a huge benefit to us. It was kind of a weird conversation initially. The idea of working with a direct competitor was certainly new for Clorox. The form and structures of a joint venture were totally undefined." It would mean a close partnership in one category, while maintaining intense competition with one another in other categories.

To Weedman, it meant finding a powerful new how-to-win choice. It meant innovation in its broadest sense. There were good licensing bids from several other companies. But going into business with Clorox would send an important signal externally—and internally—about how P&G would do business in the future. "When most people talk innovation, they think molecules," Weedman says. "This would be innovation of the business model— innovation across the whole spectrum."

With strong encouragement from the top, Weedman created a joint venture with Clorox, one in which Clorox, rather than P&G, was in control. In exchange for both of the P&G technologies and the assignment of twenty P&G personnel (mainly R&D scientists and technologists) to the joint venture, P&G received 10 percent of the overall Glad business, with an option to acquire another 10 percent on preset terms. But Clorox would run the business—manufacturing, distribution, sales, advertising, and so forth. With this deal, P&G relinquished control in a way it had never done before.

The venture was launched in January 2003, and by December 2004, P&G happily exercised the option of purchasing an additional 10 percent of the business. At the time of the joint-venture agreement, Glad was a $400 million business; within five years, it grew to more than $1 billion, boosted by the strength of Press'n Seal (the rebranded Impress) and especially ForceFlex. As important as the financial contributions of the deal were to P&G, the fundamental approach was even more important. It sent a powerful signal about the P&G of the future. This wasn't the old Procter that had to have control and had to dominate. This collaboration with a competitor—building a successful leading business in a non-competitive space—was huge. And the approach has led to a number of similar joint development initiatives, like Tide Dry Cleaners franchises, in which P&G partners in unexpected ways.

With the development of these new film-wrap technologies, P&G was faced with a series of choices about where to play and how to win. The challenge was to find a way to win, rather than just compete, with these new technologies. Finding the answer meant taking a new and creative approach to what winning could mean and how P&G could win in a different way. The how-to-win choice had to be made thoughtfully with an understanding of the full playing field. The result was a first-of-its kind partnership between P&G and Clorox—a partnership that made both companies stronger and created a billion-dollar, category-leading brand.

Where to play is half of the one-two punch at the heart of strategy. The second is how to win. Winning means providing a better consumer and customer value equation than your competitors do, and providing it on a sustainable basis. As Mike Porter first articulated more than three decades ago, there are just two generic ways of doing so: cost leadership and differentiation (for more on the micro-economic foundations of these two strategies, see appendix B).

Low-Cost Strategies

In cost leadership, as the name suggests, profit is driven by having a lower cost structure than competitors do. Imagine that companies A, B, and C all produce widgets for which customers will gladly pay $100. The products are comparable, so if one company charges more for its product than the others do, most customers will elect not to buy it in favor of the less expensive versions. Company B and company C have comparable cost structures and produce the widgets for $60, earning a $40 margin. Company A has a lower cost structure for producing essentially the same product and is able to do so for $45, producing a $55 margin. In this instance, company A is the low-cost leader and has a dramatic advantage over its competitors.

The low-cost player doesn't necessarily charge the lowest prices. Low-cost players have the option of underpricing competitors, but can also reinvest the margin differential in ways that create competitive advantage. Mars is a great example of this approach. Since the 1980s, it has held a distinct cost advantage over Hershey's in candy bars. Mars has chosen to structure its range of candy bars such that they can be produced on a single super-high-speed production line. The company also utilizes less-expensive ingredients (by and large). Both of these choices greatly reduce product cost. Hershey's and other competitors have multiple methods of production and more-expensive ingredients and hence higher cost structures. Rather than selling its bars at a lower price (which is nearly impossible because of the dynamics of the convenience-store trade), Mars has chosen to buy the best shelf space in the candy bar rack in every convenience store in America. Hershey's can't effectively counter the Mars initiative; it simply doesn't have the extra money to spend. On the strength of this investment, Mars moved from a small player to goliath Hershey's main rival, competing for overall market share leadership.

Dell Computer took a similar tack early on. In its first decade, Dell enjoyed a substantial low-cost advantage over its competitors in the PC space. Superior supply chain and distribution choices created a cost differential of approximately $300 per computer in Dell's favor; it simply cost Dell's competitors more to make, sell, and distribute personal computers. Rather than keeping all of that margin advantage, Dell returned some to consumers, underpricing its competitors for roughly equivalent products. On the strength of these lower prices, Dell gained leading market share in record time, taking a huge bite out of Gateway, HP, Compaq, and IBM in the process. The $300 margin differential gave Dell a massive winning advantage at the time. The company grew from Michael Dell's dorm-room start-up in 1984 to a company worth $100 billion at its height in 1999.

While all companies make efforts to control costs, there is only one low-cost player in any industry—the competitor with the very lowest costs. Having lower costs than some but not all competitors can enable a firm to stick around and compete for a while. But it won't win. Only the true low-cost player can win with a low-cost strategy.

Differentiation Strategies

The alternative to low cost is differentiation. In a successful differentiation strategy, the company offers products or services that are perceived to be distinctively more valuable to customers than are competitive offerings, and is able to do so with approximately the same cost structure that competitors use. In this case, companies A, B, and C produce widgets and all do so for $60 per widget. But while customers are willing to pay $100 for widgets from company A or B, they are willing to pay $115 for company C's widgets, because of a perception of greater quality or more-interesting designs. Here, company C has a $15 higher margin than its competitors and a substantial advantage over them.

In this type of strategy, different offerings have different consumer value equations and different prices associated with them. Each brand or product offers a specific value proposition that appeals to a specific group of customers. Loyalty emerges where there is a match between what the brand distinctively offers and the consumer personally values. In the hotel industry, for instance, one consumer would have a much higher willingness to pay for a service-oriented offering, like Four Seasons Hotels and Resorts, while another would more highly value a unique, boutique experience, like the Library Hotel in New York. Differentiation between products is driven by the activities of the firm: product design, product performance, quality, branding, advertising, distribution, and so on. The more a product is differentiated along a dimension consumers care about, the higher price premium it can demand. So, Starbucks can charge $3.50 for a cappuccino, Hermès can charge $10,000 for a Birkin bag, and they can do so largely irrespective of input costs.

Not all differentiators look the same. While Toyota is sometimes considered a lost-cost player because of its focus on manufacturing effectiveness, it is really a differentiator. Its manufacturing effectiveness is necessary to make up for its production environment (which is heavily weighted to high-cost Japan). However, the automaker is able to earn a price premium of several thousand dollars per vehicle over its competitors in the US car market, while producing vehicles at similar cost. The best-selling Camry and Corolla models have a reputation for superior quality, reliability, and durability, driving the significant price premium. This differentiation advantage means that when it wants to gain market share, Toyota can cut its prices without destroying profitability—and its competitors won't have the resources to respond. Or Toyota can invest some of the premium to add new, desirable features to its vehicles. In doing so, it can actually reinforce its differentiation advantage.

All successful strategies take one of these two approaches, cost leadership or differentiation. Both cost leadership and differentiation can provide to the company a greater margin between revenue and costs than competitors can match—thus producing a sustainable winning advantage (figure 4-1). This is ultimately the goal of any strategy.

FIGURE 4-1

Alternative winning value equations for low-cost strategies and differentiation strategies

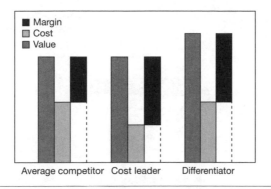

Though there are just two generic strategies, firms have many ways to employ them. In fact, in limited cases, firms can employ both strategies at the same time—driving a significant price premium over competitors and producing at a lower cost than those same competitors. This dual-strategy approach is rare, but it is possible if the company has an overwhelming share advantage and substantial scale-sensitive costs. IBM, at the height of its dominance of the mainframe computer business, is a historic example. Google and eBay are examples in the current era. P&G, in certain businesses like laundry detergents, feminine care, and fragrances, is a differentiator with cost advantages driven by market leadership and global scale. Typically, though, because markets are dynamic and new competitors find unexpected and innovative ways to deliver value, the companies that pursue low-cost and differentiation at the same time are eventually forced to choose (as IBM was, when Hitachi and Fujitsu Microelectronics entered mainframe computing with much lower cost strategies or as eBay has been forced to do, in the face of Craigslist and other alternatives).

FIGURE 4-2

Differing imperatives under low-cost strategies and differentiation strategies

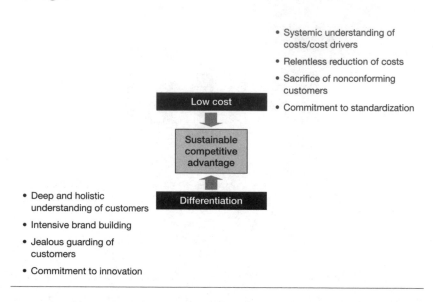

It is very difficult to pursue both cost leadership and differentiation, because each requires a very specific approach to the market (figure 4-2).

In other words, life inside a cost leader looks very different from life inside a differentiator. In a cost leader, managers are forever looking to better understand the drivers of costs and are modifying their operations accordingly. In a differentiator, managers are forever attempting to deepen their holistic understanding of customers to learn how to serve them more distinctively. In a cost leader, cost reduction is relentlessly pursued, while in a differentiator, the brand is relentlessly built.

Customers are seen and treated very differently. At a cost leader, nonconforming customers—that is, customers who want something special and different from what the firm currently produces—are sacrificed to ensure standardization of the product or service, all in the pursuit of cost-effectiveness. At a differentiator, customers are jealously guarded. If customers indicate a desire for something different, the firm tries to design a new offering that the customers will adore. And if a customer leaves, the departure drives a stake in the heart of the firm, indicating a failure of the strategy with that customer. It is as simple as the difference between Southwest Airlines and Apple. If, as a customer, you say to Southwest, "I really would like advance seat selection, interline baggage checking, and to fly into O'Hare not Midway when I go to Chicago," Southwest will say, "Great, you should try United Airlines." At Apple, if customers say, "Wow, this iPad is beautiful," Apple will take that as a cue to bring out an even prettier next-generation iPad.

Both cost leadership and differentiation require the pursuit of distinctiveness. You don't get to be a cost leader by producing your product or service exactly as your competitors do, and you don't get to be a differentiator by trying to produce a product or service identical to your competitors'. To succeed in the long run, you must make thoughtful, creative decisions about how to win. In doing so, you enable your organization to sustainably provide a better value equation for consumers than competitors do and create competitive advantage.

Competitive advantage provides the only protection a company can have. A company with a competitive advantage earns a greater margin between revenue and cost than other companies do for engaging in the same activity. A firm can use that additional margin to fight those other companies, which will not have the resources to defend themselves. It can use that advantage to win. Low cost and differentiation seem like simple concepts, but they are very powerful in terms of keeping companies honest about their strategies. Many companies like to describe themselves as winning through operational effectiveness or customer intimacy.

These sound like good ideas, but if they don't translate into a genuinely lower cost structure or higher prices from customers, they aren't really strategies worth having. Across its categories and markets, P&G pursues branded differentiation strategies that allow it to command price premiums.

Multiple Ways to Win

In the last decade, the concept of winner-take-all strategies has gained traction and credibility. It has been used prominently in connection with Toyota, Walmart, and Dell, but also applied to Microsoft, Apple, and Google. The notion is that the company in question finds *the* killer way to compete and generates such scale that the company can continue to press its advantage until it takes the entire market. Yet, long after being declared a winner who took all, Walmart experienced the rise of Target on one front and Dollar Stores on another. Dell was eclipsed in market share by a resurgent HP and is now threatened by tablets (including iPads) on the high end and inexpensive imports like Lenovo and Acer on the low end. And while Toyota is still a contender for leadership in the tough global automotive industry, it has less than a 15 percent share. Microsoft is facing stiff competition from tablets and smartphones that run alternative operating systems. Apple is competing hard with Android. Google is in a struggle with Facebook. And of course, Google and Apple now compete with each other. There simply is no one perfect strategy that will last for all time. There are multiple ways to win in any almost any industry. That's why building up strategic thinking capability within your organization is so vital.

Strategic capability is required for thinking your way out of difficult positions—like the one that faced the Gain laundry detergent team. At one point, Gain was virtually out of business—with distribution in just a few southern states. In fact, in the late 1980s, the Gain brand manager, John Lilly, sent a memo to then-CEO John Smale recommending that the brand be discontinued. Smale sent the memo back to Lilly with his full response written across the top: "John, one more try please." Smale didn't dispute the logic of the memo; he just wanted to give Gain another chance, even if it was a long shot.

The Gain team (then led by subsequent brand manager Eleni Senegos) set out to redefine the Gain where-to-play and how-to-win choices, giving it one more try. Again, the team started with the consumer. Tide was the overwhelming market leader and largely owned the all-purpose-cleaning position. But the consumer segmentation data showed that a small but passionate group of consumers wasn't well served by Tide or by any other competitive product. This segment cared very much about the sensory laundry experience—about the scent of the product in the box, the scent during the washing process, and especially the scent of clean clothes. Scent was the proof of clean for these consumers. At the time, there wasn't a brand positioned for *scent seekers*, people who want a dramatic and powerful fragrance experience from the moment the box is opened through the entire wash process, out of the dryer, and into the drawer. Gain could fill that niche.

Moving Gain into the scent-seeker position was possible through P&G's expertise with fragrance across product categories. P&G, as we've noted, is the largest fragrance company in the world; not only does it have a robust business in fine fragrances, but virtually every P&G product has a distinctive fragrance, geared to create a unique and desirable user experience. The scent-seeker positioning played to P&G's ability to create scents that are robust at all of those points in the process, and to make that clear in every way. The package was totally changed to be bright, loud, and in-your-face. It really says that if you like big, bold scents, this is the product for you. The Gain team plugged away at that positioning on the shelf and in advertising. Gain is now one of P&G's billion-dollar brands, even though it is only sold in the United States and Canada. And the impetus was Smale's push to think again, to find a new way to win.

The Febreze strategy offers another example of finding a way to win. P&G had struggled to reinvigorate its home-care business and grow the category overall. The company once held a strong position in surface cleaners, with brands like Comet and Spic 'n Span, but had made a where-to-play choice to divest those brands and refocus the home-care team on new consumer and product segments and new product technologies, building these organically rather than through acquisition. One of those new products, based on a proprietary technology, was a spray that could remove odors from soft surfaces. It wasn't a totally new product, but really a better air freshener—one that could actually remove odors rather than covering them up.

Unfortunately, the air-freshener segment had two large incumbent players in Reckitt-Benckiser (maker of Air Wick) and SC Johnson (Glade). This was a core strategic category for both companies; they weren't willing to sell their established brands to P&G and it was a category they would likely defend at all costs against a new entrant. So, in terms of how to win, the question was how best to introduce this new technology in a way that would prove its effectiveness to consumers, build a strong, differentiated brand, and avoid the competitive walled cities in air-freshening and deodorizing at the outset.

Ultimately, Febreze was a product technology in search of a job to be done. To have the best chance to win, the home-care team elected to start in P&G's home court, with laundry—positioning the new technology as a laundry additive that would attack odors. The team then attacked sequentially along the lines of least to more resistance: as a refresher for curtains, carpets, and upholstery around the home; as a deodorizer for other malodorous objects around the home, like running shoes and sports equipment; and finally as an air deodorizer and freshener. Along the way, P&G acquired AmbiPur from Sara Lee to expand the superior Febreze technology faster into Europe and certain emerging markets. Overall, it took a decade to build Febreze to leadership where it chose to play.

The fine-fragrances business, as detailed in chapter 3, is another example of the power of integrated where-to-play and how-to-win choices. P&G fell into the fine-fragrance business through an acquisition, but once there, the company thought long and hard about how to win. Rather than accept the rules of the game (a highly seasonal business with a push-and-churn approach to brands and little opportunity to bring P&G's consumer insights, brand building, and go-to-market capabilities to bear), the fine-fragrances team found new ways to win. Like the home-care team, it attacked in an area of least resistance—men's fragrances and younger, sportier scents, rather than in the heart of the most intense competition in women's prestige brands. The team found new ways to win by creating brands based on specific consumer needs and wants, partnering in distinctively successful ways with fragrance houses and designers. In doing so, the fine-fragrance business became part of P&G's larger how-to-win strategy, another way to differentiate brands along a dimension that consumers care about and to leverage the benefits of global scale.

It is tempting to believe that strategy in general, and where-to-play and how-to-win choices in particular, are needed only for outward-facing functions—those folks who interact with external consumers and competitors. But every line of business and function should have a strategy—one that aligns with the strategy of the company overall and decides where to play and how to win specifically for its context. At P&G, corporate functions are all tasked with crafting their own strategies in this way. Joan Lewis, global consumer market knowledge officer, explains: "Where to play and how to win has been a very important framework for us. Organizations are often good at one or the other without realizing that they're two different sets of decisions. At one point, we weren't as disciplined about our where-to-play choices. It was everywhere anybody needed consumer insight or anywhere we thought it could add value. Just like a business dilutes its focus and in turn its growth potential when you try to do too many things at a time or do things that are further away from your core strengths, we were relatively diluted in the nature of the impact we could have."[4]

So, Lewis and her team worked to think more critically about their strategy, considering "what kinds of company decisions or individual business decisions we are aiming to influence: those where consumer understanding is a key driver for company success. We made a clear where-to-play commitment to the company. Then we structured how to win, how to deliver against our where-to-play commitment," Lewis recounts. "The way I think of our how-to-win, from an organizational standpoint, is in two parts. One is the actual capability in the specific kinds of consumer and market research and test methods we use to answer business questions. Then, what is the best organizational structure to deliver—how much is embedded in the business, how much is corporate, what is scaled, and what is highly tailored?" P&G could have hired a leading research agency and outsourced everything. Instead, because consumer insights are so crucial to its how-to-win choices as a company, P&G kept the intellectual capital in-house, where Lewis's group designs new and customized test methods to suit specific needs, and outsources industry-standard research, like surveys and focus groups. Lewis and her team determine what winning looks like for their function, keeping their internal customers and the full marketplace in mind. This approach enables them to make smarter day-to-day decisions on the basis of an overriding strategy and to build the strongest consumer-insights capability in the industry.

The best-of-breed outsourcing strategy for P&G's GBS demonstrates the power of thinking through where to play and how to win for an internal function. The best-of-breed approach was a thoughtful choice—for each service, the company selected the provider that could best create joint value with P&G, while freeing up the core GBS team to focus on building decisive P&G capabilities. This foundational how-to-win choice has led the team to continue to focus on how to win with its internal customers—driving costs of the system, outsourcing noncore activities, and building systems to support P&G's company, business-unit, and functional strategic choices.

Reinforcing Choices

Where-to-play and how-to-win choices do not function independently; a strong where-to-play choice is only valuable if it is supported by a robust and actionable how-to-win choice. The two choices should reinforce one another to create a distinctive combination. Think of Olay, in which the new where-to-play (thirty-five- to forty-nine-year-old women interested in age-defying skin-care products) was perfectly matched with the new how-to-win (in the high-end masstige segment with mass-retail partners and products that fight the seven signs of aging). With Bounty, narrowing where to play to North America enabled the team to decide how to win around North American consumers' different needs. In the Glad joint venture, some where-to-play choices (like creating a new P&G wraps and trash bags category) would have made it difficult to win with consumers, given the nature of competition in the category and the likely response of competitors. Instead, the company found a how-to-win choice, a joint venture with a competitor, and the venture created new value for consumers and for both P&G and Clorox. The where and how were considered together, and a very different approach was created.

The P&G diaper business in emerging markets provides another example. By 2000, the company was making good progress on expanding into emerging markets across a number of categories. The baby-care business had a global strategy that included regaining brand clarity in North America, reasserting market leadership in Europe, and extending beyond diapers into other kinds of baby-care products. Launching into emerging markets was one part of this larger strategy. The decision was made to start with Asia, because of its attractive demographics. But what kind of a how-to-win choice would work well with that where-to-play choice? How could P&G not only enter the Asian baby-care market, but also win there? And how would the emerging-market strategy fit into the global baby-care strategy?

It would be a challenge. The Pampers diapers that were sold globally were simply too expensive to be sold in emerging markets. Traditionally, consumer goods companies have taken one of two approaches in such a situation. One is the trickle-down technology approach, basically taking a once cutting-edge but now largely obsolete product from the developed world and selling it in emerging markets. The other common approach is to take the existing premium product and strip out as many costs as possible. Essentially, explains Deb Henretta, then group president for Asia and global specialty (now group president of global skin care, beauty, and personal care), "we would take a diaper that at the time in North America or Western Europe was costing about

$0.24 a diaper and whittle it down, slicing the salami thinner and thinner and thinner to get to something that was in the $0.08 to $0.10 range."[5] Usually, the resulting product was deficient, a pale imitation that met no one's needs. Instead of trying either of these routes, Henretta and her team took a different approach: "Let's go to a white sheet of paper," she told her team, "keeping the consumer in mind. Let's find out what those consumers actually need and build *that* diaper. You only build what they need; you don't build all the bells and whistles that only consumers in developed markets expect."

Henretta set specific parameters for success: "We decided we wanted a baby diaper to be the cost of an egg. At that price, it would be affordable for consumers. We dovetailed that with a strategic positioning that baby diapers help control disease by providing better health and hygiene for the child, plus provide a better night's sleep for the baby. All that came together as the proposition."

The new, blank-sheet-of-paper approach required a different way of thinking about innovation capability. Traditionally, in diapers and elsewhere, the emphasis had been on cutting-edge technology. Here, the R&D teams had a different challenge—to address the specific, differentiated needs of consumers in emerging markets within specific cost parameters. It was a different way of thinking about and using the core innovation capability—but one on which the R&D teams were able to deliver. The result was market leadership in China in a rapidly growing category.

Summing Up

In choosing where to play, you must consider a series of important dimensions, like geographies, products, consumer needs, and so on, to find a smart playing field. How-to-win choices determine what you will do on that playing field. Because contexts, like competitive dynamics and company capabilities, differ greatly, there is no single, simple taxonomy of how-to-win choices. At a high level, the choice is whether to be the low-cost player or a differentiator. But the *how* of each strategy will differ by context. Cost leaders can create advantage at many different points—sourcing, design, production, distribution, and so on. Differentiators can create a strong price premium on brand, on quality, on a particular kind of service, and so forth. Remember that there is no one single how-to-win choice for all companies. Even in a single market, it is possible to compete in many different ways and succeed. Choosing a how-to-win approach is a matter of thinking both broadly and deeply, in the context of the playing fields available to the company.

Action consistent with the how-to-win choice is vital. Cost leadership and differentiation have different imperatives that should lead to different sets of activities within a firm. Structuring a company to compete as a cost leader requires an obsessive focus on pushing costs out of the system, such that standardization and systemization become core drivers of value. Anything that requires a distinctive approach is likely to add cost and should be eliminated. In a differentiation strategy, costs still matter, but are not the focus of the company; customers are. The most important question is how to delight customers in a distinctive way that produces greater willingness to pay.

Where to play and how to win are not independent variables. The best strategies have mutually reinforcing choices at their heart. As a result, it is not a matter of choosing where to play and then how to win and then moving on. Though we have placed these two choices in separate chapters for the sake of clarity, they are intertwined and should be considered together: what how-to-win choices make sense with which where-to-play choices? And which combination makes the most sense for your organization? From there, the next step is to understand the capabilities that will be required to support the where-to-play and how-to-win choices.

HOW-TO-WIN DOS AND DON'TS

- ✓ Do work to create new how-to-win choices where none currently exist. Just because there isn't an obvious how-to-win choice given your current structure doesn't mean it is impossible to create one (and worth it, if the prize is big enough).

- ✓ But don't kid yourself either. If, after lots of searching, you can't create a credible how-to-win choice, find a new playing field or get out of the game.

- ✓ Do consider how to win in concert with where to play. The choices should be mutually reinforcing, creating a strong strategic core for the company.

- ✓ Don't assume that the dynamics of an industry are set and immutable. The choices of the players within those industries may be creating the dynamics. Industry dynamics might be changeable.

- ✓ Don't reserve questions of where to play and how to win for only customer-facing functions. Internal and support functions can and should be making these choices too.

- ✓ Do set the rules of the game and play the game better if you're winning. Change the rules of the game if you're not.

PAMPERS: P&G'S SINGLE MOST IMPORTANT STRATEGIC LESSON

by A.G. Lafley

Back in the late 1950s, a P&G chemist named Vic Mills had a profound dislike for cleaning his grandson's cloth diapers; he was convinced there had to be a better way and began studying the nascent disposable-diaper product segment, which then represented less than 1 percent of the billions of diaper changes in the United States every year.

After studying first-generation disposable baby diapers from around the world, and after several designs failed in premarket consumer tests, P&G tested a three-layer, rectangular pad design (a plastic back sheet, absorbent wadding material, and water-repellent top sheet) in Peoria, Illinois, in December 1961. It failed too. Mothers liked the disposable diaper product, but the $0.10-per-diaper price was too high. After another six market tests, further refinements in design and engineering, and the development of an entirely new manufacturing process, P&G finally had a success—this time at $0.06 a diaper.

The company launched the new diaper as Pampers.[a] Throughout the rest of the 1960s and the 1970s, Pampers built significant unit volume and dollar sales by converting cloth-diaper users to disposables users. P&G effectively created a new category and easily won a leading share in it. Looking back, the Pampers story is a great example of strategic insight and vision. A better product fulfilled an unmet consumer need, delivered a better user experience, and created better total consumer value. In Peter Drucker's terms, Pampers disposable baby diapers "created customers" and served them better than competitors did.

By the mid-1970s, Pampers had achieved a 75 percent share in the United States and had been expanded to about seventy-five countries worldwide.

Imagine what Pampers could have become, then, had P&G chosen a different strategy in 1976. That's when it introduced a second diaper brand, Luvs, which featured an hourglass-shaped pad with elastic gathers. Luvs delivered superior fit, absorbency, and comfort for about a 30 percent price premium to Pampers. The decision to launch Luvs with a better product might have been the most unfortunate strategic miscalculation in P&G history. So why did P&G introduce a new brand rather than improving or extending the existing brand? First, company practice at the time dictated a multibrand strategy—a new brand for every new product in each category—and the approach seemed to be working well in laundry detergents and several other categories. Second, the new design would drive higher operating costs and required considerable investment in manufacturing capital; projections suggested that a 20 percent retail price premium would be needed to hold margins, and the company worried that current users would reject a premium-priced line of Pampers. So, Pampers stayed the same and the advanced design was introduced at the premium price as Luvs.

Unfortunately, the company had miscalculated. While consumers virtually always say they won't buy (or even try) an improved product if it is sold at a higher price, those same consumers often change their minds when the product and usage experience are clearly better and the price premium still represents value. This turned out to be the case with shaped diapers, and Pampers suffered. Then, a new threat emerged. In 1978,

Kimberly-Clark introduced Huggies, a new brand with a Luvs-like hourglass shape, a better fit, and an improved tape fastening system. On the strength of its new product, Huggies surged to a 30 percent market share. Meanwhile, the introduction of Luvs did little to bring new consumers to P&G. Instead, it split the Pampers market share between two brands. P&G still sold more diapers overall, but Pampers and Luvs individually ranked behind Huggies in market share.

Future CEO John Pepper, who had assumed control for the US operation around this time, recalls a series of focus groups that left him "in a cold sweat." Every single mom using Huggies, Luvs, or Pampers preferred the shaped diaper. Mothers had decided. So, finally, did P&G. In 1984, CEO John Smale approved the decision to move Pampers to the shaped diaper design as well. P&G launched Ultra Pampers, a design with the hourglass shape, a new, proprietary absorbent gel, a leak-proof waist-shield, elastic leg gathers, and a breathable leg cuff. The company invested $500 million in capital to build and run new diaper lines and another $250 million in marketing and sales promotion. Ultra Pampers was a success, in the sense that it converted most Pampers users to the new-generation product design and moved Pampers back ahead of Luvs in market share. But it did not provide a definitive win against Huggies in the United States; nor did it resolve the tension between Pampers and Luvs—two virtually identical products that P&G struggled mightily (but unsuccessfully) to differentiate with advertising for another decade. Finally, in the 1990s, Luvs was repositioned as a simpler, more basic value offering.

CEO Ed Artzt summarized the lessons of the Pampers story in a strategy class he taught in the early 1990s:

1. Determine whether a product innovation is really brand specific or ultimately category generic. Never give your current brand user a product-based reason to switch away. By denying Pampers the hourglass shape and better-fit features for a decade, the brand lost five generations of new parents and new babies.

2. Competition will follow your technology, trying to at least match it and ideally beat it. Technical superiority alone is not sustainable.

The Luvs shaped diaper wasn't the only strategic challenge to beset Pampers over the years. In the late 1980s, P&G decided to pass on pull-on diapers. Instead, Huggies developed Pull-Ups training pants, creating and taking leadership of a large, new segment. The trainers commanded premium pricing per change and accounted for a disproportionate share of Kimberly-Clark's baby diaper profits, allowing it to compete more effectively in the taped-diaper segment as well. In Asia, Unicharm similarly rode pull-on pad technology to leadership in the baby-diaper category in its home market of Japan and subsequently in several other Asian countries.

As John Pepper recounts in his book *What Really Matters*, the decision not to invest in pull-ons in the late 1980s was made because P&G was still under intense pressure to get its Ultra Pampers product upgrade execution right.[b] The company succumbed to the first-things-first argument and put every available resource on fixing the current problem. It did not balance returns from the present with investing in the future. Again, P&G miscalculated on consumer preferences, over-weighted concerns about capital and price premium, and underestimated the competition. In the end, if P&G had just taken the time to understand consumers, it would have embraced pull-ons and turned the last two decades into a three-way competition in that segment.

The P&G baby diaper saga is full of strategic challenges occasioned by disruptive product designs and technologies, by very different readings of the consumer, and by competitors' strategic choices that changed the game. But it is still a winnable category for P&G, with the right strategic thinking. Pampers today is an $8 billion business with a leading share of the $25 billion global disposable baby diaper market (over 30 percent, versus Kimberly-Clark's Huggies, with around 20 percent share), in large part because of P&G diaper leadership in Europe and other markets, where the company stayed single-mindedly focused on the Pampers brand franchise. The business is a significant engine of growth and value creation. Sometimes, P&G has gotten it right.

In all my business life, I have never seen any more competitive industry than baby care. Consumers are demanding and discriminating, and they turn over quickly—it's a whole new consumer base every three years. Baby diapers are one of the most expensive items—if not the most expensive item—in a parent's shopping basket every week. Competition is intense. Retailers are competitors; virtually every major retailer targets young families as a prime prospect, and most offer their own private-label brand of diapers. The market is big and growing steadily in emerging markets, where there is a huge potential to serve babies who will begin life using cloth or no diapers at all. The bets are big too; this is a high-capital business where product and machine obsolescence is a continual threat. It demands winning choices that sustain competitive advantage long enough to produce significant value creation. The baby diapers war will go on. The best strategies will win.

a. The Pampers story has been told several times from different vantage points. See Oscar Schisgall, *Eyes on Tomorrow* (Chicago: G. Ferguson, 1981), 216–220; Davis Dyer, Frederick Dalzell, and Rowena Olegario, *Rising Tide: Lessons from 165 Years of Brand Building at Procter & Gamble* (Boston: Harvard Business School Press, 2004), 230–239; and John E. Pepper, *What Really Matters: Service, Leadership, People, and Values* (New Haven, CT: Yale University Press, 2007).

b. Pepper, *What Really Matters*.

Chapter Five

Play to Your Strengths

Most corporate mergers fail to create value. The bigger the deal, the less likely it seems to produce success. There are many cautionary tales, including AOL Time Warner, DaimlerChrysler, Sprint-Nextel, and Quaker-Snapple. In each instance, promised synergies failed to materialize, value was destroyed rather than created, and shares plummeted. In the case of Snapple, Quaker paid $1.7 billion for the brand in 1995, promising to turn it into the next Gatorade. Less than three years later, Quaker unloaded a much-diminished Snapple for just $300 million. Time Warner valued AOL at approximately $190 billion at the time of their merger and just ten years later spun it off for a mere $3 billion.[1]

So how did P&G's 2005 acquisition of Gillette manage to buck the trend? The merger was no simpler. In fact, it was relatively complex, as the *Sunday Times* of London explains: "$11 billion of Gillette sales combined with $57 billion of P&G business, 30,000 employees combining with 100,000 at P&G, on the ground in 80 countries, selling in 160."[2] Yet, the acquisition delivered over $2 billion in cost synergies in two years and continues to deliver significant revenue synergies after integration. Gillette was P&G's

biggest value-creating acquisition by a wide margin, comfortably exceeding the value creation promised to shareholders.

The roots of the acquisition's success go back to the initial consideration of the opportunity. As Clayt Daley, who retired as chief financial officer in 2009, explains, P&G had three relevant criteria for any acquisition. First, any acquisition had to be "growth accretive—in a market that was growing (and likely to continue growing) faster than the average in its space and in a category or segment, geography or channel where we thought that we could grow as fast as the market, if not faster."[3] This was the first, and most obvious, hurdle. Second, the acquisition had to be structurally attractive—a business "that tended to have gross and operating margins above the industry or company average. We were looking for businesses that could generate strong, free cash flow." Free cash flow was an important driver of value creation for P&G corporately. Once those two hurdles were cleared, there was a final criterion—one that too few companies consider systematically: how the potential acquisition would fit with the company's strategy—its winning aspiration, its choices about where to play and how to win, its capabilities, and its management systems.

Gillette had powerful brands (like Mach 3, Venus, and Oral B) that would importantly add to the P&G beauty and personal-care businesses. And it contributed significant cash flow. But, as Daley explains, "then you get into 'what did P&G bring to the party? How good of a fit are they with our sources of competitive advantage?'" The fit was quite good: in terms of where to play, Gillette provided the leading male and female shaving brands and the leading toothbrush business in the world, all large enough to instantly become core businesses for P&G. Gillette also fit well with the strategic choice to grow in the beauty-care and personal-care categories. Plus, geographically, it offered complementary strengths in emerging markets, providing leadership positions in countries where P&G was building presence (like Brazil, India, and Russia). On how to win, Gillette's brand-building expertise, product innovation, core technologies, and retail merchandising mastery aligned well with P&G's company-level choices.

But there was still more to consider. "At the end of the day," Daley continues, "it really comes down to, are you, as an acquirer, going to bring value to that acquisition or not? The acquisition is only really successful if you're a better owner of the business than either the previous owner or the company as an independent company. That usually gets down to your capabilities, in our case, your consumer capabilities, your branding capabilities, your R&D capabilities, your go-to-market capabilities, your global infrastructure, your back office. Are the capabilities and strengths that you're bringing to the business going to improve it, grow it faster, and create more value than it did before?" In short, strategic fit between the new business and P&G capabilities was critical.

Gillette and the Strategic Choice Cascade

Chip Bergh, then P&G's president of men's grooming, oversaw the Gillette global business unit (GBU) integration (along with Bob McDonald, who led the global market development organization [MDO] integration and Filippo Passerini, who led back-end integration). Bergh recalls, "Unlike a lot of acquisitions, it wasn't a successful company buying an unsuccessful company. It was a successful company buying a successful company."[4] Bergh was the first P&G person on the ground at Gillette, heading to Boston just ten days after the deal closed. "A big part of my job initially was helping Gillette plug into P&G, connecting the pipes, making sure that everything was working, keeping the business going, and working with the Gillette CEO, Jim Kilts, and the leadership team, while also learning their business from them."

Nine months later, Bergh officially took over the blades and razors business. First, "we went to work on Gillette's male grooming strategy," he recalls. "There was a lot to love about the business, but I felt that there was a lot of opportunity too. I wanted to use an off-site with the leadership team to send a signal that we've got to protect all of the great things that have worked, but then start really bringing to the party some of P&G's core capabilities. We were looking for ways that we could accelerate growth on this very profitable and attractive business." It was a matter of leveraging Gillette and P&G capabilities and selectively creating new ones where capabilities did not exist at the level required to win.

As discussed earlier, the five capabilities core to P&G's where-to-play and how-to-win choices are consumer understanding, brand building, innovation, go-to-market ability, and global scale. The notion of bringing these capabilities to bear on the Gillette business was top of mind. From the first meeting post-acquisition, Bergh set out to incorporate P&G's strategy framework into the Gillette DNA, working to articulate Gillette's choice cascade. Once the where-to-play and how-to-win choices were clear, the team could turn its attention to the capabilities required to deliver on those choices.

Soon an explicit where-to-play and how-to-win strategy for Gillette as part of P&G emerged. The first choice was to get back into a clear-cut winning position with male shaving systems, leveraging Gillette Fusion, a top-end product about to be launched. The second was to extend the Gillette brand into men's personal-care items, like deodorants and shampoo, building on P&G's innovative beauty and personal-care product technologies. Third was to win in women's hair removal too, across wet shaving, epilators, and depilatories. The fourth strategic priority for Gillette was to stimulate consumption by expanding into emerging markets in general and to India in particular.

Gillette would need specific capabilities to deliver on these choices. As with diapers, a where-to-play choice that included the developing world demanded a thoughtful how-to-win choice suitable for that context. Gillette needed a razor that would uniquely meet the needs of consumers in the developing world. To get there, the team would have to bring P&G's deep consumer understanding and world-leading innovation into play.

P&G's deep-dive ethnographic approach to consumer research (which relies on in-store and in-home observation and qualitative assessments) was largely new to Gillette, which had relied much more heavily on standard quantitative research. Bergh encouraged his team to think differently about the emerging-market consumer. He recalls a meeting in Boston that launched Gillette's first-ever design-from-scratch innovation for emerging markets, with a focus, in this case, on India. The group included, he says, "scientists from the Reading Technical Centre in the UK, our upstream innovation lab outside of London, scientists from Boston, marketing people, and market-research people, all together for a three-day session to start mapping out the work."

Bergh's direction to the team was simple: "The first thing I want you to do is to spend two weeks in India. I want you to live with these consumers. I want you to go into their homes. You need to understand how they shave and how shaving fits into their lives." One of Gillette's senior scientists, a research fellow from the Reading lab, was, according to Bergh, both highly respected and conceptually brilliant. Bergh says the scientist wasn't convinced: "He raised his hand, kind of sheepishly, and said, 'Chip, why do we have to go to India? We have a lot of Indian men who live right outside of our door in Reading. Why can't we just recruit them?'"

Why indeed? Yet Bergh was convinced that going to India was the right things to do. His experiences told him it would be necessary to engage with real Indian consumers on the ground in the

actual Indian market. So he sent the team to India. He was grati-
fied by the result: the same scientist sought him out a few months
later during an innovation review. Bergh recalls the man's words:
"'Now I completely get it,' he said, 'You can look at pictures in
the books, you can hear the stories, but it's not until you're there
[that you understand]. I spent three days with this one guy, shopping with him, going to the barber shop with him, watching him
shave. Now I really understand the company's statement of purpose about improving consumers' lives . . . I was so motivated and
so inspired, I designed the first razor on a napkin flying back to
London." The man, Bergh says, had tears in his eyes as he told the
story.

Only in India did the scientist really begin to understand the
needs of the Indian consumer. He learned what he could not learn
inside his lab or from consumer testing outside London. Typically,
razors are designed and tested with the assumption that everyone
shaves as people do in the West, with reliable access to a large sink
and running hot water. In India, the team members saw that this
simply wasn't true. Many of the men they met shaved with only
a small cup of cold water. Without hot running water to clean the
razor, small hairs tend to clog the blade, making shaving far more
difficult. Gillette's new product would take that unique challenge
into account. It would be a new kind of razor, custom-built to
meet the needs of consumers in India. The Gillette Guard razor,
as it came to be called (and which bore a close resemblance to the
one first sketched on that napkin), has a single-blade system with
a safety comb designed to prevent nicks and an easy-rinse car-
tridge.[5] The razor costs 15 rupees, or $0.34, and uses blades that
cost 5 rupees, or $0.11, to replace.[6] By contrast, the top-end Gil-
lette Fusion Pro-Glide is sold for $10.99 in the United States,
with replacement blade cartridges at about $3 each.[7] Within three
months, the Guard was the best-selling razor in India, winning

through a set of capabilities in innovation and consumer under-standing that had to be cultivated, rather than left to chance. By engaging directly with the Indian consumer, by treating that con-sumer as the boss, the Gillette team was able to understand what he values and what he experiences.

For chief information officer Passerini, the capabilities required to make the Gillette acquisition a success looked a little different. For him and his team, the whole undertaking was in large part a sys-tems-integration challenge. They had to integrate two massive busi-nesses, with two very different IT systems, without missing a beat. "We integrated Gillette in fifteen months," he says, with just a hint of pride in his voice. "That was worth $4 million per day, doing it in fifteen months instead of doing it in the usual three to four years."[8] The accomplishment required that Passerini apply P&G's capabili-ties to his own IT infrastructures—thinking about scale and innova-tion in a new way. Passerini set about innovating his team structures, his partnership models, indeed his whole business, to take advantage of scale rather than be trapped by it. He created a flow-to-the-work model whereby most of his organization had project-based rather than permanent assignments. This structure enabled his massive IT team to be nimble and innovative, efficient and effective. The team members had the skills needed to integrate the systems; Passerini created a structure that supported them in doing so.

In determining whether to make the acquisition, we thought long and hard about how Gillette's strategy would fit with P&G's. We wanted to determine whether there could be a real strategy for the combined business, a clear plan to win. We saw cultural compatibility between the two companies: they shared the same aspirations to win and core values. We also believed that P&G and Gillette could work productively together and that the business and external work systems could be fully integrated in a relatively short period. We believed the acquisition could deliver value from cost synergies and future growth. Typically, in an acquisition, all the focus is on integration, on synergies, and on getting the right leadership in place. But synergy is not strategy.

Strategy mattered most. We believed that P&G and Gillette were a good strategic fit and that Gillette's capabilities married well with P&G's. We believed that P&G could leverage that common ground to build new capabilities where it needed them. On the strength of all that, the huge, bet-the-company-size acquisition of Gillette made sense. It took some time to convince all the stakeholders. But it was clear that this could be a once-in-a-century strategic opportunity, if P&G brought the right capabilities to bear on it.

Understanding Capabilities and Activity Systems

An organization's core capabilities are those activities that, when performed at the highest level, enable the organization to bring its where-to-play and how-to-win choices to life. They are best understood as operating as a system of reinforcing activities— a concept first articulated by Harvard Business School's Michael Porter. Porter noted that powerful and sustainable competitive advantage is unlikely to arise from any one capability (e.g., having the best sales force in the industry or the best technology in the industry), but rather from a set of capabilities that both *fit* with one another (i.e., that don't conflict with one another) and actually *reinforce* one another (i.e., that make each other stronger than they would be alone).

For Porter, a company's "strategic position is contained in a set of tailored activities designed to deliver it."[9] He calls the visual depiction of this set of activities an *activity system*. Since "competitive strategy is about being different . . . [and] means deliberately choosing a different set of activities to deliver unique value," an activity system must also be distinctive from the activity systems of competitors.[10] In his landmark 1996 article "What Is Strategy?," Porter illustrated his theory with examples from Southwest Airlines, Progressive Insurance, and The Vanguard Group, articulating the way in which each organization made distinctive choices and tailored an activity system to deliver on those choices.

The activity system is a visual representation of the firm's competitive advantage, capturing on a single page the core capabilities of the firm.[11] Articulating a firm's core capabilities is a vital step in the strategy process. Identifying the capabilities required to deliver on the where-to-play and how-to-win choices crystallizes the area of focus and investment for the company. It enables a firm to continue to invest in its current capabilities, to build up others, and to reduce the investment in capabilities that are not essential to the strategy.

In 2000, P&G's where-to-play choices were coming together (i.e., grow from the core; extend into home, beauty, health, and personal care; and expand into emerging markets), and its how-to-win choices were also becoming clear (i.e., excellence in consumer-focused brand building; innovative product design; and leveraging global scale and retailer partnerships). These choices needed to be translated into the set of capabilities required to deliver.

The thinking process was kicked off at an off-site meeting for business and functional leaders. Leaders were placed into teams by business and by function and then asked to capture what they thought were the key strengths of the company. After a long day of discussion and debate, the teams had generated more than a hundred potential competitive strengths on charts around the room. As might have been predicted, every function had identified its unique set of disciplinary capabilities and competencies. Every business had identified capabilities that were unique to its industry.

The question needed to be reframed. The next morning, everyone would be given three votes on what constituted the core capabilities of the company, along the following criteria: first, for a given capability, the group had to be reasonably sure P&G already had real, measurable competitive advantage in that area and could widen its margin of advantage in the future. Second, the capability had to be broadly relevant and important to the majority of P&G's businesses. That is, it had to be a company-level rather than business-level capability that distinguished P&G from its competitors. Third, the capability had to be decisive, a real competitive advantage that was the difference between winning and losing. Ultimately, the question was, what capabilities must P&G, as a global company, have to win across the industries in which it would compete?

With capabilities, again, winning is an essential criterion. Companies can be good at a lot of things. But there are a smaller number of activities that together create distinctiveness, underpinning specific where-to-play and how-to-win choices. P&G certainly needs to be good at manufacturing, but not distinctively good at it to win. On the other hand, P&G does need to be distinctively good at understanding consumers, at innovation, and at branding its products. When articulating core capabilities, you need to distinguish between generic strengths and critical, mutually reinforcing activities. A company needs to invest disproportionately in building the core capabilities that together produce competitive advantage.

When thinking about capabilities, you may be tempted to simply ask what you are really good at and attempt to build a strategy from there. The danger of doing so is that the things you're currently good at may actually be irrelevant to consumers and in no way confer a competitive advantage. Rather than starting with capabilities and looking for ways to win with those capabilities, you need to start with setting aspirations and determining where to play and how to win. Then, you can consider capabilities in light of those choices. Only in this way can you see what you should start doing, keep doing, and stop doing in order to win.

Back at the retreat, after a good night's sleep and with time to reflect on clearer criteria, the group came to five core capabilities:

1. *Understanding consumers.* Really knowing the consumers, uncovering their unmet needs, and designing solutions for them better than any competitor can. In other words, making the consumer the boss in order to win the consumer value equation.

2. *Creating and building brands.* Launching and cultivating brands with powerful consumer value equations for true longevity in the marketplace.

3. *Innovating (in the broadest sense).* R&D with the aim of advancing materials science and inventing breakthrough new products, but also taking an innovative approach to business models, external partnerships, and the way P&G does business.

4. *Partnering and going to market with customers and suppliers.* Being the partner of choice by virtue of P&G's willingness to work together on joint business plans and to share joint value creation.

5. *Leveraging global scale.* Operating as one company to maximize buying power, cross-brand synergies, and development of globally replicable capabilities.

Once the capabilities were articulated, the team then spent most of the day deciding how and where to begin investing in each capability to broaden and deepen competitive advantage. It wrote an action plan for each of the five capabilities to create competitive advantage at the corporate, category, and brand levels.

These capability choices would guide P&G's strategic choices for the next decade. The five P&G capabilities can be understood as forming the basis of P&G's company-level activity system. In our adaptation of Porter's original concept, the activity system captures the core capabilities required to win, the relationships between them, and the activities that support them; this map supports where-to-play and how-to-win choices, as shown in figure 5-1.

In this system, the core capabilities are shown as large nodes, and the links between the large nodes represent important reinforcing relationships. These reinforcing relationships make each

FIGURE 5-1

Procter & Gamble activity system

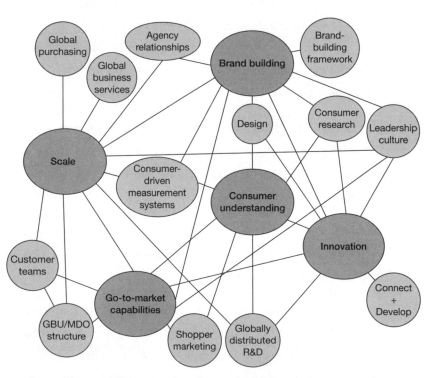

Connect + Develop is P&G's open-innovation program; see also chapter 6. *Abbreviations*: GBU, global business unit; MDO, market development organization.

capability stronger, which is an essential characteristic of an activity system: the system as a whole is stronger than any of the component capabilities, insofar as those capabilities fit with and reinforce one another. For instance, there is a close connection between consumer understanding and innovation. For P&G, innovation must be consumer centered if it is to be meaningful and provide competitive advantage—so innovation requires a deep understanding of the needs of consumers. The goal is to connect consumer needs with what is technologically possible. Innovation is also connected to go-to-market capabilities. New innovative products keep retail channel partners excited about P&G and reinforce the close relationship between the company and its best customers—but only if P&G takes care to think of both retailers and end consumers during the R&D process. A great new product for consumers is of little use to P&G if it can't be shelved and sold effectively within retail channels. And of course, innovation can also be brought to bear on retail relationships, improving in-store merchandising and supply-chain efficiencies.

The subordinate nodes are the activities that support the core capabilities. Scale, for instance, is supported by the way in which P&G is structured. At P&G, GBUs oversee categories, brands, and products, providing a holistic, consistent approach to each element on a worldwide basis. At the same time, MDOs have responsibility for a continent, region, country, channel, or customer, paying close attention to its specific needs and demands. The GBUs and MDOs work together to create a global approach with local applicability and customization. This matrix allows P&G to drive scale where it is needed but to stay nimble on the ground. Scale is also supported by global purchasing and global business services. Scale also enables, and is supported by, customer teams (i.e., teams who work solely with specific customers, like Tesco or Walmart), agency relationships (P&G has the largest ad budget in the world), and consumer- and customer-driven measurement systems (qualitative and quantitative approaches to understanding and reporting performance). Through the sheer size and volume of activity, P&G is able to afford more resources than competitors in each of these areas—and to get better performance.

An activity system is of no value unless it supports a particular where-to-play and how-to-win choice. Again, the various choices along the cascade must be considered iteratively. You need to go back and forth between the choices. You can think through a tentative where-to-play and how-to-win choice. Then you can ask, what activities system would effectively underpin this choice? Once you lay out such a system map, you can ask a sequential set of questions about feasibility, distinctiveness, and defensibility.

In addressing feasibility, ask several questions: is this a realistic activity system to build? How much of it is currently in place, and how much would you have to create? For the capabilities you would need to build, is it affordable to do so? If upon reflection, you find that the activity system isn't feasible, then you need to reconsider where to play and how to win.

When you have a feasible activity system, you can ask more questions: is it distinctive? Is it similar to or different from competitors' systems? This is an important point. Imagine that a competitor has a different where-to-play and how-to-win choice, but a very similar set of capabilities and supporting activities. In such a situation, the competitor could shift to your potentially superior where-to-play and how-to-win choices and begin to cut in to your competitive advantage. If the activity system isn't distinctive, the where and the how and the map must be revisited until such time as a distinctive combination emerges. As Porter notes, not all of the elements need to be unique or impossible to replicate. It is the combination of capabilities, the activity system in its entirety, that must be inimitable.

When it has a feasible and distinctive activity system, you can ask, is the system defensible against competitive action? If the system can be readily replicated or overcome, then the overall strategy is not defensible and won't provide meaningful competitive advantage. In that case, you need to revisit your where-to-play and how-to-win choices to find a set of strategic choices and an activity system that are difficult to replicate and hard to defend against.

The goal, then, is an integrated and mutually reinforcing set of capabilities that underpin the where-to-play and how-to-win choices and that are feasible, distinctive, and defensible. Measuring the P&G activity system against these criteria, it fairs well. Time has demonstrated that it was feasible to build: some capabilities, such as Connect + Develop (P&G's version of open innovation), design, globally distributed R&D, and the global business services organization, had to be built, so P&G invested in them. The activity system as a whole is distinctive. While competitors have some of the capabilities, none has the entire combination that P&G has. L'Oréal has powerful brands and innovative design, but a fraction of P&G's scale. Unilever has similar scale but doesn't have P&G's global go-to-market capability, because of Unilever's country-based rather than global organizational structure. No competitor invests as much in consumer understanding or product innovation—and has introduced so many new products across so many categories. Finally, the activity system has been defensible: no competitor has been able to replicate the entire system map or outperform against the full set of capabilities. Note, however, that this does not mean P&G has an obviously superior strategy. As we have noted before, there are many ways to play in any industry. There are numerous where-to-play and how-to-win choices, backed by core capabilities, in any field of competition. In the consumer-goods industry, P&G's strategy is but one of the successful ones.

Capabilities Throughout the Organization

If you are in a business that has one product line or brand, you may well have a single set of core capabilities and one activity system for the whole company. In a corporation, though, with different brands, categories, and markets, each different business line makes its own where-to-play and how-to-win choices within the context of organizational choices. Logically, then, each unit must have an activity system that supports its choices, a system that is informed by the corporate-level map. In other words, layers of capabilities occur throughout the organization, and the activity systems look at least a little different in different parts of the company.

At P&G, the activity system for baby care differs from the systems for laundry or skin care. Hospital sampling programs and relationships with nurses and health systems are important supporting activities to a baby-care choice to capture new moms early. There is no direct parallel to that activity in skin care or laundry. In the same way, the laundry team doesn't need to develop relationships with fashion editors and dermatologists (for independent credentialing and endorsements) as the skin-care team does. And the activity systems for the global business services organization or the European MDO would look different from the brand and category systems.

However, if there is nothing in common between these different activity systems, it is a sign that the organization has businesses that may fit poorly in the same portfolio. For a corporation to have a chance of delivering greater value together than the units could individually, there must be some core activities in common—both among businesses in the portfolio and between those businesses and the company overall. It is essential that all of the systems have at least some capabilities and activities that line up with the core capabilities of the organization. These shared capabilities—the ones that run through multiple divisions or units and the organization overall—create *reinforcing rods* that link different parts of the organization together, just as steel reinforcing rods run from floor to floor in a concrete building to keep it standing (figure 5-2). These reinforcing rods help drive strategy forward at all levels.

Again, although the baby-care, laundry, skin-care, GBS, and European MDO activity systems will be distinct from one another and from the P&G system in some respects, they will each have some crucial reinforcing rods that tie their capabilities together. For instance, all five of P&G's company-level core capabilities are important for the baby-care business. Scale and innovation are critical to GBS, which oversees IT and other central services. Go-to-market capabilities are obviously critical to the European MDO, but so too are consumer understanding and scale. As discussed, P&G's consumer insights, innovation, and scale were important for Gillette. The links between the systems are crucial

FIGURE 5-2

Reinforcing rods

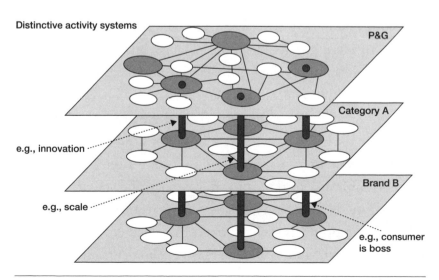

to create brand, category, sector, function, and overall company competitive advantage—to make the system stronger than the sum of its parts.

Multilevel Strategy

Given that core capabilities exist at different levels of the organization, it is hard to know just where to start thinking about them—with corporate strategy or with business strategy. Ultimately, there is no perfect place to start and the process isn't linear—you need to go back and forth between the levels, just as you need to loop back and forth between the five questions in the strategic choice cascade. However, you can use three principles to help the company put together integrated activity systems at multiple organizational levels.

1. Start at the Indivisible Level

When building an activity system, you will know that you are in the right spot if the following conditions hold true: (1) the activity system would look more or less the same down one level, but (2) it looks meaningfully different up one organizational level. In the case of Head & Shoulders, for instance, one level down from brand would be individual product (Head & Shoulders Classic Clean, Head & Shoulders Extra Volume, and so on). If you were to build the activity system for each of these products and compare it with the brand system, there would be little difference. Each product represents a small variation in formulation. But going up a level from brand to the hair-care category, the activity systems would be quite different. At the hair-care category level, the portfolio includes products such as Nice 'n Easy hair colorants, Herbal Essences hair gels, and so on. The Head & Shoulders map is geared to produce advantage via innovation in therapeutic ingredients, while the Nice 'n Easy map prominently features implements, dispensers, and color research. The hair-care category activity system would need to be a more general system that captures the essence of those below it and connects to those above.

The ground-level maps (e.g., Head & Shoulders and Nice 'n Easy) can be thought of as *indivisible activity systems*: below this level, the activity system doesn't divide into distinct maps, while above this level, multiple distinct maps are aggregated together into a unique system. This indivisible level will not be the same in every organization (i.e., the indivisible activity system is not always found at the brand level). Every company has to find the level of direct competition and begin articulating capabilities there. Build activity systems starting at the ground level—the point of indivisible activity systems—and work your way up from there. Why? The capabilities at the indivisible level drive the ones above.

2. Add Competitive Advantage to the Level Below

All levels above the indivisible activity system are aggregations that must add net competitive advantage in some way. Since aggregation inevitably creates costs (financial and administrative) that wouldn't exist if the indivisible activity systems existed as separate businesses, the strategy at all levels of aggregation must contribute a countervailing benefit to those below, somehow improving their competitiveness.

A level can contribute a net benefit in two ways—through two kinds of reinforcing rods. First, it can provide the benefit of a shared activity. For example, the hair-care category can have a research laboratory that does fundamental research on cleaning, conditioning, and styling, which, because of its massive scale across all the hair brands, performs at a fraction of the cost that it would take for Head & Shoulders to do on its own. The technology advantage that is enabled through shared activities can be powerful. The second way a higher level of aggregation can provide value is through skills and knowledge transfer. For example, if Head & Shoulders needs well-trained brand managers and R&D managers to work in its business, and those can be provided by the hair-care category, then this represents a valuable transfer of skills to Head & Shoulders.

Management at the each level of aggregation should seek to develop an activity system that focuses as exclusively as possible on the key reinforcing rods through which that level has chosen to add value to the levels below it. The aggregator's primary job is to help the level below compete more effectively through shared activities and transfer of skills. This means having a clear view of how the level wishes to add value and then focusing all of its resources on doing so. Activities that don't add value to activity systems below should be minimized, because they destroy value. For example, only if the hair-care category can demonstrate value (from sharing of activities and transfer of skills) that is greater than the financial and administrative costs that it imposes on Head & Shoulders, Nice 'n Easy, Pantene, Herbal Essences, and so forth, should it exist as a level of aggregation in the corporation. Otherwise, the level should be eliminated.

3. Expand or Prune the Portfolio Below to Enhance Competitiveness

While the first job of each aggregation level is to develop capabilities that support those levels below, the second job is to expand and prune the lower-level portfolio on the basis of fit to broader capabilities. With respect to enhancing the portfolio, consider the organizational reinforcing rods—the capabilities that run through and create advantage in the whole of your organization—and determine whether the portfolio can be expanded into other businesses that would benefit competitively from those reinforcing rods. The creation of the Swiffer and Febreze brands within P&G's

home-care category are excellent examples of expanding a portfolio according to advantaged reinforcing rods in consumer understanding and innovation. Without the ability to understand unmet consumer needs and innovate against them, neither product would exist today.

Equally important is pruning of the portfolio below when the benefits of the reinforcing rods cannot match the financial and administrative costs of aggregation. These are businesses that would be better off in another company's portfolio or as independent operations. P&G aggressively pruned businesses for which its five corporate capabilities couldn't assist substantially in generating competitive advantage, divesting about fifteen businesses a year for ten years, between 2000 and 2009. Big, profitable brands such as Folgers and Pringles had to go because they were not going to benefit from company reinforcement enough to sustain competitive advantage over the long term. Both had built strong brands, but had limited opportunity for product innovation within P&G's mass channels of distribution.

Gillette: Reinforcing Rods

Why was the Gillette acquisition so successful for P&G? The answer is reinforcing rods; the P&G reinforcing rods drove powerfully through Gillette's activity system, especially in its crown jewel, the male shaving business. Strengths in all five core capabilities enabled P&G to add value to the core Gillette business. By bringing Gillette into the P&G portfolio, P&G was able to add real value by sharing and transferring those capabilities.

Consider scale: both P&G and Gillette are major global advertisers. Given the sheer size of Gillette's media budget, you could imagine that becoming part of P&G would have little effect on its advertising costs. But as it turned out, P&G could replicate

Gillette's premerger advertising program at 30 percent less, because of P&G's additional size and spending advantage. As the largest advertiser in the world, P&G confers the costs savings that accrue from that position to Gillette.

In terms of go-to-market capability, P&G was able to fold the Gillette brands into the multifunctional customer teams at the world's largest retailers, gaining both cost efficiencies and additional leverage with the retailers. P&G also transferred its industry-leading joint value-creation practices to Gillette, wherein P&G works directly with retailers to design and implement customer programs and partnerships that benefit both the retailers and P&G.

In consumer understanding and innovation, P&G brought to bear advanced consumer research techniques and a more globally dispersed innovation capability to enhance the level and quality of innovation (as with the new razor for the Indian market). Plus, the GBS team innovated in terms of structures and processes to finish the integration quickly and effectively, minimizing costs and frustration.

Of course, Gillette had its own capabilities that could strengthen P&G's capabilities during and after the integration. Gillette is one of the best in the world at launching new products, leveraging targeted marketing, and in-store merchandising to generate high levels of consumer trial. It was also advantaged in its in-store display capabilities, adapting its visuals and shelving approach effectively in almost any format or space in a store. Acquiring Gillette helped P&G up its own marketing and merchandising games.

Already a great company, Gillette was a successful acquisition because it benefited dramatically from the five core capabilities of P&G. An additional advantage was that Gillette already had substantial capabilities of its own in those areas. The fit was very good for the men's and women's shaving businesses and Oral B, and pretty good for Duracell. Braun (Gillette's electric shaver and small-appliance business) presented challenges. It didn't benefit as directly from P&G consumer understanding, R&D, and mass retail distribution. The difference between the value created with male shaving on one end of the spectrum and Braun on the other illustrates the importance of reinforcing rods in multilevel, multi-category businesses.

Supporting the Choices

From the where-to-play and how-to-win choices follows the next question: what capabilities are required to deliver on that strategy? To understand and visualize those capabilities, you will find it helpful to prepare an activity system based on the strategy. An activity system captures the most important activities of the organization in a single visual representation. The large nodes of the map are the core capabilities, while the smaller nodes are the activities that support those core capabilities.

The activity system should be feasible, distinctive, and defensible if it is to enable you to win. If the system is missing any of these three qualities, you need to return to the where-to-play and how-to-win choices, refining or even entirely changing those choices until they result in a distinctive and winning activity system.

By identifying the capabilities required to achieve competitive advantage, the firm can apply resources, attention, and time to the things that matter most. There may well be work to do to bolster and grow those capabilities, including training and development, investing in additional resources, building supporting systems, and even reorganizing the company around the capabilities. The process of creating systems that support the specific choices and capabilities of the organization will be examined in the next chapter.

BUILDING CAPABILITIES DOS AND DON'TS

✓ Do discuss, debate, and refine your activity system; creating an activity system is hard work and may well take a few tries to capture everything in a meaningful way.

✓ Don't obsess about whether something is a core capability or a supporting activity; try your best to capture the most important activities required to deliver on your where-to-play and how-to-win choices.

✓ Don't settle for a generic activity system; work to create a distinctive system that reflects the choices you've made.

✓ Do play to your own, unique strengths. Reverse engineer the activity systems (and where-to-play and how-to-win choices) of your best competitors, and overlay them with yours. Ask how to make yours truly distinctive and value creating.

✓ Do keep the whole company in mind, looking for reinforcing rods that are strong and versatile enough to run through multiple layers of activity systems and keep the company aligned.

✓ Do be honest about the state of your capabilities, asking what will be required to keep and attain the capabilities you require.

✓ Do explicitly test for feasibility, distinctiveness, and defensibility. Assess the extent to which your activity system is doable, unique, and defendable in the face of competitive reaction.

✓ Do start building activity systems with the lowest indivisible system. For all levels above, systems should be geared to supporting the capabilities required to win.

Chapter Six

Manage What Matters

The last box in the strategic choice cascade is the most neglected. Often, senior management teams formulate strategy and then broadcast key themes to the rest of the company, expecting quick and definitive action. But even if you set a winning aspiration, determine where to play and how to win, and define the capabilities required, strategy can still fail—spectacularly—if you fail to establish management systems that support those choices and capabilities. Without supporting structures, systems, and measures, strategy remains a wish list, a set of goals that may or may not ever be achieved. To truly win in the marketplace, a company needs a robust process for creating, reviewing, and communicating about strategy; it needs structures to support its core capabilities; and it needs specific measures to ensure that the strategy is working. These management systems are needed to complete the strategic choice cascade and ensure effective action throughout the organization.

Systems for Making and Reviewing Strategy

Once upon a time, the strategy creation and review process at P&G was, as global home care president David Taylor describes it, "corporate theater at its best."[1] Taylor recalls his early reviews as brand manager: "There were twenty-five people around the room. There was my vice president, the president of the ad agency, and then what I'd call a whole lot of rail birds—people lined up on each side." In front of that huge audience, the brand manager was called to perform. "You'd come in with a notebook with fifty issue sheets. The idea was, whatever was asked, you had to answer. You go to tab twenty-five; you go to tab forty."

Tales abounded of a particular CEO who seemed to revel in the chance to put people on the spot with tough, detailed questions. "I can remember the stories," Taylor recalls. "Somebody told me, 'Your objective in this meeting is just to not get humiliated. Get out of it alive.' Then, when I became more senior, I had a president tell me, 'Your job in that meeting is to talk anything but strategy. Bring innovation projects, bring [advertising] copy, bring material to entertain him. You don't want him messing around with your strategy. Talk anything but strategy." This get-in-and-get-out approach became deeply embedded in the P&G culture.

We knew we had to reinvent the process entirely, to actually focus on strategy rather than on budget negotiations or product and marketing execution. We wanted to foster a team-like approach that would allow the CEO to collaborate with the presidents and to help advance their thinking in real time. We wanted to create useful dialogue in place of a one-way, bulletproof presentation. Instead of burying the issues, we wanted to talk about them openly. We wanted a new management system for the creation and review of the five strategic choices.

Longtime chief financial officer Clayt Daley, equally tired of all the sell-and-defend reviews, agreed that there must be a better way. He recalls, "Management teams, because the [P&G] culture is so strong, were trained for so many years to come in and sell. We wanted to talk about strategic options and alternatives and what things we could plug in or take out of the strategy." This different approach came not from a desire to micromanage strategy from the top but from an understanding of the different perspectives the senior team and the business presidents could bring. We believed that the senior leadership team could leverage both its considerable expertise across businesses, functions, and geographies and its unique, enterprise-wide perspective to improve and contextualize a smart strategy developed by leaders with deep knowledge of a specific business. This combination of breadth and depth could be incredibly powerful.

Unfortunately, the management teams had been trained over decades to see strategy reviews as anything but an opportunity to share ideas. Traditionally, it had been their job to build an unimpeachable plan and to defend it to the death. It was important to reframe the task or, as Daley puts it, "to create a framework of what a strategy discussion is and isn't. A strategy discussion is not an idea review. A strategy discussion is not a budget or a forecast review. A strategy discussion is how we are going to accomplish our growth objectives in the next three to five years. We really wanted to engage in a discussion."

So we worked up a new process to begin in the fall of 2001. It was a radical change for all involved. Previously, a president would come into a review meeting with a lengthy PowerPoint presentation, which captured all the material that he or she wanted to share. The president would go through the deck, slide by slide, revealing the material to the mass audience in real time. We changed the meeting completely. It went from a formal presentation (by the business to management) to a dialogue focused on a very few critical strategic issues identified in advance.

Whatever strategic issues the president wanted to discuss were delivered in writing in advance of the strategy review meeting. The senior team would review the submission and select the issues it wished to discuss (or propose alternative points of discussion).

A one-paragraph note (and never more than a one-page letter) would go back to the president, highlighting those issues for discussion. Some meetings focused on a single strategic question, and the team rarely tried to wrestle with more than three questions in a single meeting. The culture-busting kickers were threefold. First, there would be no presentation, only a discussion of the strategic issues agreed on in advance. Second, we limited the number of folks in the room, down from twenty-five to just four or five from the business plus the CEO and the corporate leaders who would bring specific experience or knowledge on the strategy issue. Third, participants would not be allowed to bring more than three new pages of material to the meeting to share—we did not want the participants to race off and create yet another PowerPoint deck with answers to the questions raised in the letter. We genuinely wanted to have a conversation about the key strategic issues in the business.

The questions tended to press on a few key points: was P&G winning in this category? Was the business team sure? How did they really know? What were the opportunities related to unmet consumer needs? What were the most promising innovations and technologies? What were the threats to category or country or channel structural attractiveness? What core capabilities was the business lacking? What was its most troubling or threatening competitor? These reviews focused on very basic, very fundamental questions with the intent of helping the team make better strategic choices. The group would spend three or four hours chewing on the few critical issues together.

We had three reasons for the shift in process. First, we wanted to shift the culture of the organization to one that was more dialogue oriented. Second, we wanted to create a structure in which the business teams could truly benefit from the experience and cross-enterprise perspective of senior leaders. And finally, we wanted to build the strategic-thinking capabilities of P&G's executives, asking them to practice thinking through strategic issues with others in real time. P&G executives are great operators in the businesses and the functions. The company needed its leaders to become better strategists because better, more choiceful strategies would enable yet better operations. P&G needed multidimensional leaders who could both make tough strategic calls and lead effective operating teams. The company would need more of these multidimensional leaders to win in an increasingly complex, global, and competitive world. So, strategy reviews were redesigned to work individual and collective strategic muscles.

The change created a good deal of angst at first. Slowly but surely, though, the review meeting became what we hoped it would be: an inquiry into the competitiveness, effectiveness, and robustness of a strategy. In due course, the presidents came to understand that they wouldn't be judged on whether they had every aspect of their strategy buttoned up but rather on whether they could engage in a productive conversation about the real strategic issues in their business. As a result, P&G leaders began to do more strategic thinking, to have more strategic conversations—not just at strategy reviews, but in the normal course of business—and the quality of strategic discourse improved. More importantly, the company saw better choice making, more willingness to make hard calls, and eventually better business results.

The new system was a stark contrast to the theater that David Taylor had been used to: "A.G.'s role was to elevate my thinking and my team's thinking to come out with a better strategy than we came in with." Freed from an obligation to sell a perfect plan or to try to impress the boss, Taylor started to enjoy these meetings. He had the chance, he says, "to engage in a conversation with really smart people. It became nonthreatening to have a conversation and not have all the answers, because A.G. didn't attack. If he disagreed, he would do it in a very thought-provoking way . . . The tone of the meeting was very conversational and engaging. We sat down, talked, handed things [across the table]." Looking back, he says, the dynamic was tied to the questions at the heart of strategy: "The whole feel of the meetings . . . they weren't about how we deliver the forecast this year or how we deliver the forecast next year. It wasn't about profit or people or other short-term issues. They were about, where are you going to play and how are you going to win?"

Melanie Healey, now group president North America, was also an enthusiast for the new process:

What we would do is agree up front with A.G. on the key strategic issues that he wanted to have us address in these meetings—in addition, of course, to the strategic topics we wanted to talk about . . . The [meetings] actually worked very well, because there were never any big, huge surprise discussions that we were unprepared for. Given we had agreement to the subjects ahead of the meetings, we made sure that with the prereading we'd send out ahead of time, everyone had sufficient background to engage in a productive dialogue, add value, and provide outstanding input on the critical strategic elements we needed help on. We always came out of these meetings with some terrific builds on our strategic choices from very experienced leaders in the company.[2]

Of course, no process is flawless and no remedy can satisfy every user. One president, a terrific leader and strategist, was less impressed with the new format, which he saw as difficult to implement in his mature business, a less-than-perfect fit with P&G's

achievement culture, and potentially uncomfortable for participants, including himself:

> *The meetings themselves, although A.G. tried to make*
> *them true work sessions—where we think through options,*
> *where we think through the business landscape and the*
> *choices we could make and why this alternative choice is*
> *better than the other and all that—they rarely got to that*
> *in-depth, true strategic conversation. It's not because A.G.*
> *didn't try; it's because frankly the culture of P&G got*
> *in the way. If I am the president of the business and I'm*
> *sitting across from A.G. and his lieutenants, I am not going*
> *to make myself vulnerable by saying, "Hey, here are the*
> *four things we looked at. This is what we think we should*
> *do, but what do you think?" A.G. was very engaged at*
> *the strategy-creation level, but the most value I got from*
> *him was in one-on-one, more intimate settings, rather than*
> *the kind of formal, annual forums when you have a big*
> *audience and a big group of people.*[3]

These concerns show how difficult it can be to make a wholesale shift. Yet, concerns notwithstanding, there was a distinct shift
in the quality and utility of the strategy review meetings within a
couple of cycles. By 2005, the new approach to strategy reviews
was so ingrained and viewed by the majority as so superior to the
prior system that it would have been inconceivable to go back.

The strategy dialogue went on at all levels of the organization,
returning again and again to choices of where to play, how to win,
competitive core capabilities, and management systems. Presidents had to submit a monthly letter directly to the CEO and had
a monthly or (at minimum) quarterly meeting, either in person or
on the phone. The ongoing discussion helped keep the strategy on

track and helped give the CEO insights into the strategic capabilities of his leaders. In the regular one-on-one meetings, the first part of the agenda belonged to the president. The strongest presidents leveraged the time to tackle real issues and collaborate on the answers, rather than for show and tell.

New Norms for Dialogue

In any conversation, organizational or otherwise, people tend to overuse one particular rhetorical tool at the expense of all the others. People's default mode of communication tends to be advocacy—argumentation in favor or their own conclusions and theories, statements about the truth of their own point of view. To create the kind of strategy dialogue we wanted at P&G, people had to shift from that approach to a very different one.

The kind of dialogue we wanted to foster is called *assertive inquiry*. Built on the work of organizational learning theorist Chris Argyris at Harvard Business School, this approach blends the explicit expression of your own thinking (advocacy) with a sincere exploration of the thinking of others (inquiry). In other words, it means clearly articulating your own ideas and sharing the data and reasoning behind them, while genuinely inquiring into the thoughts and reasoning of your peers.

To do this effectively, individuals need to embrace a particular stance about their role in a discussion. The stance we tried to instill at P&G was a reasonably straightforward but traditionally underused one: "I have a view worth hearing, but I may be missing something." It sounds simple, but this stance has a dramatic effect on group behavior if everyone in the room holds it. Individuals try to explain their own thinking—because they do have a view worth hearing. So, they advocate as clearly as possible for their own perspective. But because they remain open to the possibility that they may be missing something, two very important things happen. One, they advocate their view as a possibility, not as the single right answer. Two, they listen carefully and ask questions about alternative views. Why? Because, if they might be missing something, the best way to explore that possibility is to understand not what others see, but what they do not.

Contrast this to managers who come into the room with the objective of convincing others they are right. They will advocate their position in the strongest possible terms, seeking to convince others and to win the argument. They will be less inclined to listen, or they will listen with the intent of finding flaws in other arguments. Such a stance is a recipe for discord and impasse.

We wanted to open dialogue and increase understanding through a balance of advocacy and inquiry. This approach includes three key tools: (1) advocating your own position and then inviting responses (e.g., "This is how I see the situation, and why; to what extent do you see it differently?"); (2) paraphrasing what you believe to be the other person's view and inquiring as to the validity of your understanding (e.g., "It sounds to me like your argument is this; to what extent does that capture your argument accurately?"); and (3) explaining a gap in your understanding of the other person's views, and asking for more information (e.g., "It sounds like you think this acquisition is a bad idea. I'm not sure I understand how you got there. Could you tell me more?"). These kinds of phrases, which blend advocacy and inquiry, can have a powerful effect on the group dynamic. While it may feel more forceful to advocate, advocacy is actually a weaker move than balancing advocacy and inquiry. Inquiry leads the other person to genuinely reflect and hear your advocacy rather than ignoring it and making their own advocacy in response.

We actively fostered this approach to communication at P&G, encouraging dialogue in the strategy review sessions, in one-on-one meetings, and all the way to the boardroom. The goal was to create a culture of inquiry that would surface productive tensions to inform smarter choices. The explicit goal was to create strategists at all levels of the organization. Over the course of a career, P&G leaders gain practice designing strategy for brands and products lines, categories, channels, customer relationships, countries and regions, and functions and technologies. The idea is to build up strategy muscles over time, in different contexts, so that as managers rise in the organization, they are well prepared for the next strategic task. As they succeed, the reward is a bigger, tougher, and more complex strategic challenge. This practice-makes-perfect approach to learning strategy explains why so many P&G alums go on to become CEOs.

Though P&G has a strong culture of individual achievement, leaders also recognize the importance of teams to the development of strategy. No individual, and certainly not the CEO, would try to craft and deliver a strategy alone. Creating a truly robust strategy takes the capabilities, knowledge, and experience of a diverse team—a close-knit group of talented and driven individuals, each aware of how his or her own effort contributes to the success of the group and all dedicated to winning as a collective.

Taking a group of individual high achievers and asking them to work together to craft strategy is no simple matter. Since strategic choice is a judgment call in which nobody can prove that a particular strategy is right or the best in advance, there is a fundamental challenge to coming to organizational decisions on strategy. Everyone selects and interprets data about the world and comes to a unique conclusion about the best course of action. Each person tends to embrace a single strategic choice as the right answer. That naturally leads to the inclination to attack the supporting logic of opposing choices, creating entrenchment and extremism, rather than collaboration and deep consideration of the ideas.

To overcome this tendency, P&G needed to create a culture of inquiry and norms of communication that allowed individuals and teams to be more rather than less productive.

A Framing Structure

In any organization, but especially in an organization as large as P&G, there needs to be a framework for organizing the strategy discussion. At P&G, a preexisting management system for describing strategy could be leveraged: the OGSM, a one-page document that captures objectives, goals, strategy, and measures for a brand, category, or company. It was a helpful tool in that it could easily be adapted to the strategic choice cascade and was a framework already well understood in the company. Unfortunately, though, the average OGSM document reads like a laundry list of initiatives rather than an articulation of the core where-to-play and how-to-win choices of the business. So, we enforced a practice by which the strategy section had to contain a clear and explicit expression of where to play and how to win, choices that connected in compelling ways with the aspirations of the business and the measures of success indicated in the final section of the OGSM. The goal was to create in the OGSM a simple, clear expression of a strategy, a living document that everyone in the business knew and understood. A new OGSM might look something like the one found in table 6-1, which is an adaptation of the real family-care OGSM from several years ago.

The OGSM became the strategic starting point for other important discussions throughout the year. At innovation program reviews, the question was, how does the product innovation portfolio fit with where you're going to play? How does it advance how you're going to win? In light of the annual operating budget and plan, the question was, are you allocating your dollars and

TABLE 6-1

A sample OGSM (objectives, goals, strategy, and measures) statement

Objectives	Strategy	Measures
Improve the lives of families by providing consumer-preferred paper products for kitchen and bathroom Be the operating TSR leader in North American tissue/towel and value creator for P&G	**Where to play:** • Win in North America • Grow Bounty and Charmin margin of leadership • Win in supermarket and mass discount channels • Build performance, sensory, and value consumer segments	• Operating TSR progress • Share and sales growth progress • Profit growth progress **Efficiency measures:** • Capital efficiency • Inventory turns **Consumer preference measures:**
Goals	**How to win:**	• Weighted purchase intent

Year-on-year operating TSR > x%
 	
x% annual share and sales growth
 	
x% annual gross and operating profit margin improvement
 	
x% return on capital investments in plant equipment and inventory
	1. Be lean
	   • Get plant/equipment capital spend to xx of sales
	   • Reduce inventory by x%
	2. Be the choice of consumers
	   • Superior base products, prices right
	   • Preferred product formats and designs
	   • Manage category growth
	3. Be the choice of retailers
	   • Improve shelf availability and service
	   • Develop differentiated shopping solutions
	   • Win with the winners
		• Trial, purchase, and loyalty
		
		Retailer feedback measures:
		• Key business drivers (distribution, share of shelf, share of merchandising, etc.)
		• Preferred vendor

your human resources toward the strategic priorities? The OGSM became the foundation of all manner of discussions, effectively grounding capital allocation, branding, resourcing, and innovation strategies in where to play and how to win.

The OGSM, new strategy review meeting structure, and inquiry culture were the foundations of P&G's new system for creating, reviewing, and communicating strategy. The OGSM enabled teams and individuals to share a strategic point of reference and to capture the most important strategy themes in a single document. The new meeting structure, as part of an annual pattern of meetings and interactions on strategy, created a new norm for communication between leaders and their teams throughout the organization. A culture of inquiry surfaced productive tensions and enabled deep conversations that advanced strategic thinking. But the company also needed mechanisms for communicating the core of the P&G strategy to the entire global organization. Rather than relying on a trickle-down method, in which the CEO communicated to presidents, who communicated to general managers, and so on, we thought long and hard about how to frame messages for the whole organization.

Communicating the Strategy

Strategy is formulated at all levels of the organization, and to be successful, it needs to be clearly communicated at all levels as well. The businesses must communicate their strategies to management (in P&G's case, through reviews and the OGSM), but management must also communicate the company-level choices to the whole organization. The challenge is to find simple, clear, and compelling ways to do so. A massive binder or thick PowerPoint deck won't rally an organization. So it is important to think explicitly about the core of a strategy and the best way to communicate its essence broadly and clearly. Ask, what are the critical strategic choices that everyone in the organization should know and understand?

At P&G, it boiled down to three themes that would enable the company to win, in the places and ways it had chosen, regardless of the details of individual differences between businesses:

1. Make the consumer the boss.

2. Win the consumer value equation.

3. Win the two most important moments of truth.

These ideas flowed directly from the corporate-level strategic choice cascade. The first dictum, that the consumer is boss, was a reorientation to the company's aspiration—to improve the lives of consumers. We wanted everyone focused on the end consumer in all aspects of the business: in innovation, branding, go-to-market strategies, investment choices, and so on. We wanted to be clear about just who the most important stakeholder is and always should be. Not shareholders. Not employees. Not retail customers. But rather the end user: the people who buy and use P&G products.

The second crucial theme was to win the consumer value equation. This quickly and unambiguously defined the way that P&G would win: by opening up a bigger gap between the value it offers to consumers and the cost of delivering that value than competitors' gaps. This meant providing unique value to consumers (through brand differentiation and innovative products). And it meant maintaining a cost position that would let P&G offer that value to the consumer at an attractive price and still make a healthy profit. This edict turned everyone's attention toward the where-to-play and how-to-win choices that create sustainable competitive advantage through differentiation.

The third and final message was the vital importance of winning the two most important moments of truth.[4] In consumer terms, the notion behind moments of truth is that a company's performance is the sum total of all its interactions with its consumers, the moments in which the brand promise is either realized or not in the consumer's mind. It is when the consumer enjoys the Gain fragrance for the first time, when Tide with Bleach actually does whiten his whites, and when Cover Girl LashBlast mascara dramatically lengthens the look of her lashes. It is when the product experience reinforces the brand promise and helps start a first-time purchaser down the path toward repurchase, regular usage, and, ultimately, brand loyalty.

The notion that there are two crucial moments of truth—when the consumer encounters the product in the store for the first time and when he or she first uses at home—was significant for P&G. Previously, the whole company had focused primarily on that second moment—the at-home, in-use moment. We wanted to highlight and elevate the significance of the first moment of truth, illustrating just how important that in-store experience is to winning. Is the product in stock? Is it prominently positioned on the shelf? Does the packaging help the consumer understand the performance promise and the value proposition? Is it merchandised in a way that reinforces the brand promise and builds on it? Does something in the merchandizing and in-store marketing compel the consumer to pick up that product, rather than the one right beside it or down the aisle? Indicating that winning would require winning both of the first two moments of truth signaled an important shift for the company. This message spoke to a broader set of capabilities as the core of a winning strategy—not just brand building and product innovation, but also retail, IT, logistics innovation, go-to-market capabilities, and the use of scale and consumer understanding to deliver the consumer value equation and drive consumer purchase.

While the messages themselves were pivotal for embedding the strategic intent in the organization, so too was the language used to convey them. It was simple, evocative, and memorable. In any organization, the choices at the top must be precisely and evocatively stated, so that they are easily understood. Only when the choices are clear and simple can they be acted upon—only then can they effectively shape choices throughout the rest of the organization. These simple strategy messages can capture the very heart of the organization's intent—and to be effective should be repeated over and over again—to different groups, in different contexts, creating a mantra for the organization.

Direct, broadcast messages to the organization are another systems tool, in addition to communication norms and formal strategy systems like OGSM and the review meetings. Together, these systems and structures can create a culture of strategic decision-making. This is one important aspect of the management systems stage. But beyond systems to support the creation, review, and communication of strategy, companies also need systems that bolster their core capabilities.

Systems to Support Core Capabilities

Every company needs systems to support the building and maintenance of its key capabilities. The capabilities, which are captured in the fourth box of the choice cascade, are so important to competitive advantage that a company needs to install systems to ensure that these capabilities are properly nurtured. The challenge is to determine what kinds of systems are needed and how best to create them. P&G created supporting systems for each of its core strengths, investing resources and attention to building sustainable structures:

- On consumer understanding, P&G invested aggressively in new consumer-research methodologies, striving to lead the industry with real in-house consumer and market research capability.

- P&G invested significantly in innovation—in understanding the innovation process, in exploring disruptive innovation with Clay Christensen and Innosight, and in creating Connect + Develop (the P&G version of open innovation), so that more than half of the company's new brand and product innovation had one or more external partners by 2008.

- P&G formalized its brand-building framework and set out to create new brands that would improve the lives of consumers. P&G introduced more brands than any other company in its industry over the first decade of the twenty-first century. Some did not achieve or sustain commercial success (like Fit, Physique, and Torengos), but the majority ended up as successful, going concerns, and some created significant new categories or segments (e.g., Actonel, Align, Febreze, Prilosec, and Swiffer).

- On the go-to-market front, P&G invested heavily in strategic partnerships with retailers. It created new ways of doing business with retail customers, suppliers, and even competitors (in noncompetitive categories), leading the charge to change the traditional business model in which all important activities exist within the walls of the firm.

- P&G invested significantly in scope and scale, articulating the ways in which the advantages they confer are more about learning curves and re-applicability than about size.

The work on scale, overseen by Clayt Daley and current chief financial officer Jon Moeller, illustrates P&G's approach to building systems around core capabilities. As Moeller explains, there was one important question on scale: "Are you capturing that value, both in terms of your activity systems and in terms of your economics? We historically weren't. If you go way back, we were really operating as individual countries. We then made an important move to go to global categories."[5] The move happened in three steps over a decade. First, under John Smale, P&G moved the majority of the US business to a category management structure. Under Ed Artzt, P&G created global category coordinators to manage technologies and brands on a more global basis. Then, under John Pepper and Durk Jager, the company moved to true GBUs—fully resourced global businesses and profit centers. "Those moves got us part of the way" to realizing the true benefits of scale, Moeller says.

"The next step," he continues, "was to ask, what are the activities that support the enterprise that really shouldn't be re-created for each global business unit? What are the activities where we can create benefit through commonality and centralization? You start with very basic things, like purchasing-spend pools. We didn't do that historically. Even advertising—each division had purchased its own advertising, which was crazy." Consolidating purchasing globally, whether for advertising or chemicals or packaging, dramatically increased P&G's scale advantage and cut costs substantially.

Moeller and Daley also looked carefully at that bane of corporate life: overhead. "We had always benchmarked ourselves to competition," Moeller recalls, "to understand whether we were efficient or inefficient on a relative basis in terms of overhead spent. It was always a straight math comparison. Clayt said, 'Wait a minute. To the extent that we're effectively scaling ourselves, we should have a lower overhead cost as a percentage of our sales.'" In other words, if there was a scale advantage at work, P&G's overhead should be significantly lower than the competition's.

Daley wanted a way to better quantify the benefits of scale to overhead efficiency. Moeller continues: "We struggled for a year or two to put together some modeling on what benefit we should see from category scale, company scale, country scale, so that we could hold ourselves accountable to a standard of overhead efficiency that was truly reflective of our scale." Because scale was a critical core competency, it was necessary to build supporting systems and to measure it in meaningful, impactful ways. It wasn't enough to merely say that scale was important.

P&G has created measurable cost advantages in several of its businesses (including laundry, fine fragrances, feminine care, and GBS). But it hasn't quite realized Daley's desire to have lower-than-average overhead as a percentage of sales across all the businesses, functions, and geographies. "That's still a journey that we're on," Moeller explains. "We've done a good job with the conceptual understanding and the modeling. But through that work, I think we did a decent job of getting intentional about creating scale." The company made changes in areas as diverse as manufacturing and currency hedging to better support corporate scale and to deliver the benefits of that scale to the business units.

"It's not enough to build scale for a brand or category," Moeller observes. "You have to integrate that into the company. The processes that you put in place to do that, they have to be very deliberate. It doesn't happen by itself. What happens [naturally] is entropy. You have to leverage scale in a way that doesn't disable entrepreneurialism, business ownership. It's integrative. It's not centralized. Centralized is a very different thing. This scale work is bringing the leaders of the businesses to work together towards a plan that not only optimizes the company, but in its best form, optimizes their category as well. As we approach a market, for instance, with multiple categories, the chance for success for each of them increases." Going into a new emerging market with several complementary categories, rather than just one, for instance, can enable cost sharing and increase local influence, thereby increasing the chance of success in the region.

Brand building, too, was a capability P&G needed to build systems to support. Though brand building had been the heart of business for more than a century, as late as 2000, the company did a poor job of capturing, cataloging, and systematically learning from brand and marketing successes and failures. Most institutional knowledge on brand building and marketing was either captured in pithy one-page memos by legendary chief marketing officers (like Ed Lotspeich or Bob Goldstein) or passed down in anecdotal storytelling by marketing masters and company leaders who had lived through the experience. The implicit message was that if young brand managers and assistant brand managers hung around seasoned brand builders long enough, these less experienced managers would master branding and marketing in due course.

So, the company launched a project to codify P&G's approach to brand building for the first time. Deb Henretta, then general manager of laundry, was the executive sponsor, and the team comprised three outstanding marketing experts: Lisa Hillenbrand, Leonora Polonsky, and Rad Ewing. Their work led to the creation of P&G's brand-building framework (BBF) 1.0, which explained P&G's approach to brand building in one coherent document for the first time. In 2003, the team updated the framework and released BBF 2.0 to the organization, followed by BBF 3.0 in 2006 and BBF 4.0 in 2012. Each version was an enhancement over the prior one in comprehensiveness, clarity, and actionability. Now, with the BBF frameworks in place, new marketers can learn the trade more quickly and senior managers have an organized and written resource to guide their efforts. The BBF and its subsequent refinements serve as a management system that nurtures and enhances the critical brand-building capacity of P&G.

We encouraged the design of systems in support of P&G's company capabilities, which were leveraged across all levels of the organization. But we also encouraged categories and brands to build systems to support the winning capabilities that were unique to their industry. These systems would prove to be decisive in some cases. Consider SK-II, P&G's super-premium skin-care line.

Though SK-II looks at first like a tenuous fit with the corporate where-to-play and how-to-win choices, it serves as an important advance guard in beauty care. What P&G learns from competing in this super-high-end segment is so valuable to the rest of the category that the company is willing to build distinctive capabilities and systems to support it. Because the brand generates extremely high gross margins, P&G can afford to invest in those unique capabilities. SK-II offers a range of skin-care products at the very top of the market and is sold through specialized counters in department stores. To win, P&G needs capabilities in consumer understanding, product and packaging innovation, and brand building—as do all of its brands. But with SK-II, P&G also needs capabilities in counter design, department store retail relationships, consumer skin consultation, and in-store service. So, the company built supporting systems, including partnerships with the best retail designers in the world, recruiting systems for beauty counselors, and training programs for in-store staff. These are all unique to SK-II, but essential to winning in that business. These systems support brand-specific capabilities, and they must be built alongside enterprise-wide systems.

Measurement of Desired Outcomes

It's an old saying that what gets measured gets done. There's more than a little truth to this. If aspirations are to be achieved, capabilities developed, and management systems created, progress needs to be measured. Measurement provides focus and feedback. Focus comes from an awareness that outcomes will be examined, and success or failure noted, creating a personal incentive to perform well. Feedback comes from the fact that measurement allows the comparison of expected outcomes with actual outcomes and enables you to adjust strategic choices accordingly.

For measures to be effective, it is crucial to indicate in advance what the expected outcomes are. Be explicit: "The following aspiration, where to play, how to win, capabilities, and management systems should produce the following specific outcomes." Expected outcomes should be noted in writing, in advance. Specificity is crucial. Rather than stating "increase in market share" or "market leadership," quantify a thoughtful range within which you would declare success and below which you would not. Without such defined measures, you can fall prey to the human tendency to rationalize any outcome as more or less what you expected. Within an organization, every business unit or function should have specific measures that relate to the organizational context and that unit's own choices. These measures should span financial, consumer, and internal dimensions, to prevent the team from focusing exclusively on a single parameter of success.

For measures at the P&G corporate level, we had identified clear financial goals, so measurement of revenue and profitability was a priority. We wanted simple, straightforward, and strong financial performance to be rewarded. However, we believed that the methodology for value creation and comparing P&G to competitors needed to change. P&G's compensation system had tied rewards for senior executives to market total shareholder return (TSR), the increase in share price plus dividends (as if reinvested in stock) over a three-year period. Under that system, the TSR was benchmarked against a peer group; if P&G was in the upper third of the group, the executives received bonuses.

We weren't satisfied with the system. We didn't like the direct tie to stock price as the sole measure of financial performance; it was too blunt an instrument to capture the real performance of the company. The stock price is a manifestation of investor expectations—something substantially out of P&G's control. After a strong year, expectations typically amp up to unrealistic levels that even a similar great performance can't beat. So, the stock will stumble, even as the company outperforms the previous year. For this reason, a great year against TSR is usually followed by a weak one, even if the company performance improves in real terms. So using this measure and basing compensation on it didn't make a lot of sense.

Instead, P&G switched from market TSR to operating TSR. Operating TSR is an amalgamated measure of three real operating performance measures—sales growth, profit margin improvement, and increase in capital efficiency. This measure more accurately captures P&G's true performance across the most critical operational metrics and, moreover, measures things that business-unit presidents and general managers can actually influence, unlike the market-based TSR number. The operating TSR measure integrates revenue growth, margin growth, and cash productivity and it does so regardless of the type of assets being managed—whether you have hard assets like tissue/towel paper converting machines or inventory like cosmetics and fragrance products. In other words, the measure could be equitably and usefully applied to all of P&G's diverse businesses. And it isn't utterly unconnected to stock performance—there is a high correlation over the medium and long term between operating TSR and market TSR. But unlike the stock price, the operating TSR measures are ones over which P&G managers have real influence in the short and medium term.

The use of operating TSR also enabled P&G to compare itself to competitors in a meaningful way; P&G could actually calculate an operating TSR for competitive firms using public data. When P&G didn't fare as well, it became an impetus to improve performance on one or more of the operating TSR drivers. Operating TSR also reduced some of the gamesmanship inherent in other systems that allow businesses to choose their own performance metrics. Having a single measure of value creation at the company and business-unit levels (and using that same measure across businesses and over time) enabled more balanced, consistent, and reliable performance.

Measures can and should be developed throughout the organization. We asked P&G leaders to think about the kinds of measures that would truly advance strategic thinking in their own businesses. Some measures were highly industry specific and were put in place in only a few P&G businesses. But other measures created or implemented in a given business spread across the organization. Some of the best thinking about cross-enterprise measures concerned understanding consumer preferences, like Henretta's work in baby care.

Like many P&G businesses, the diaper business had become a bit myopic—it was focused on technical product performance. Recalls Henretta: "Basically, we used to test how much moisture a diaper could absorb. That was the test of product superiority, and that, over time, got equated with brand superiority. The product that had the best absorbency was deemed to be the best diaper. All of our metrics over time were geared to that absorbency metric. That's how we defined success or nonsuccess. If we had a better diaper, a more absorbent, technically superior diaper, we then by definition would have the better product for consumers."[6]

But did consumers think about diapers in the same way? Henretta had her doubts: "As diapers got more and more sophisticated, moms started to expect more. It wasn't just good enough to have the technical performance" on one primary product dimension. In fact, most of the diapers on the market had quite similar levels of performance on the absorbency front. And though tests typically showed its products had superior absorbency, Pampers wasn't winning in the marketplace.

Henretta wanted to explore the other measures that might drive consumer preference, purchase, and, over time, loyalty. "We created a metric that would look holistically at all of the components that made up product or brand preference. Our weighted purchase intent (WPI) measure looked at a number of product dimensions that included things like the aesthetic appeal, the design, the feel of the diaper, the look of the diaper in addition to technical performance; it also considered the brand proposition you were giving to the consumer and the price of the product." The goal of WPI was to capture the complete picture, the full proposition as presented to consumers. It was to understand all the components of the consumer value equation: the drivers of consumer preference and the overall perceptions of product and brand value.

The WPI metric, Henretta says, "started to show where we had deficiencies. Even where we had technical superior performance, we found that we had a WPI disadvantage; when you consider all of the ways a mom evaluates a baby-care brand, we just weren't doing enough on some of the other aspects, like the feel of the diaper, the look of the diaper, the design of the diaper." The data gave Henretta the ammunition she needed to spur a change in the business: "It was an important part of making the shift, because we could show the organization, and even my leadership team, that we weren't doing as well on our diapers as we thought we were. They had this view that we had far and away the most superior diaper. They weren't taking into consideration all these other purchase factors that the consumer used when she made her decision on what brand she was going to buy; she was coming up with a very different value equation than our internal technical testing showed." WPI suggested that factors like the way the baby looked in the diaper and the ease of putting the infant in the diaper were far more important than technologists believed. "We proved, market by market, that when we used this WPI metric, we could explain the dynamics in the marketplace," Henretta says. "The WPI winner was the fastest-growing brand in the marketplace and often the market leader."

The data from the WPI analysis informed the transformation of the baby-care business, and the metric soon spread throughout P&G. WPI was just one of many measures that better helped P&G win. The company took existing best-in-class measures, adopted them, and adapted them to make them better, like using an adapted net promoter score to track consumer sentiment and loyalty.[7] The company also developed unique and proprietary test methodologies. Together, these measures were very important contributors to P&G's strategic success.

Shifting Gears

Every company needs systems to formulate, refine, and clearly communicate the essentials of the strategy choice cascade throughout the company. It needs systems to support and invest in its core capabilities. It needs systems to measure attainment of its goals. These management systems are a key piece of the strategy puzzle. While where to play and how to win represent the heart of strategy, those choices won't provide sustainable advantage without associated core capabilities that drive competitive advantage and the management systems that support the choices.

Building management systems takes time, money, and focus. There is no one-size-fits-all set of systems; they need to be geared to individual context and capabilities. Until a set of systems and measures is in place, the strategic choice cascade is incomplete and your strategy job is not done (not that it is ever truly done!).

The five choices of the strategy choice cascade summarize and define the strategy for an organization (or category or brand). Having delved into each choice to explain how it is made and having provided examples to illustrate the point, we will now step back to the broader question of how to actually make critical strategic choices. What do you need to consider to make informed choices? What should you think about, and when? How do you weigh competing and opposing options to come to a single smart choice? And how do you make these decisions in a group? These are vital questions to consider as you bring this strategy approach to your organization. They will be discussed in the next two chapters.

MANAGEMENT SYSTEMS AND MEASURES DOS AND DON'TS

- ✓ Don't stop at capabilities; ask yourself which management systems are needed to foster those capabilities.

- ✓ Do continue strategic discussions throughout the year, building an internal rhythm that keeps focus on the choices that matter.

- ✓ Do think about clarity and simplicity when communicating key strategic choices to the organization. To get at the core, don't overcomplicate things.

- ✓ Do build systems and measures that support both enterprise-wide capabilities and business-specific capabilities.

- ✓ Do define measures that will tell you, over the short and long run, how you are performing relative to your strategic choices.

COMMUNICATING TO THE ORGANIZATION

by A.G. Lafley

One of the biggest lessons I had learned in my years at P&G was the power of simplicity and clarity. I found that clearer, simpler strategies have the best chance of winning, because they can be best understood and internalized by the organization. Strategies that can be explained in a few words are more likely to be empowering and motivating; they make it easier to make subsequent choices and to take action. It was a lesson I had first learned in Asia, where I worked for eight years—three in the 1970s and five in the 1990s. Then, English was typically the second language of Asian employees. So, the simpler and clearer the language I used, the more likely it would be understood. The better the choices were understood, the more likely they would lead to action.

As CEO, I applied those lessons to the strategic direction of P&G overall. I set about communicating my choices and intent in the simplest and most compelling terms I could. To begin, I reaffirmed the company's purpose, values, and principles: to serve the world's consumers and to make the everyday lives of consumers better with P&G brands and products. I talked openly and often about integrity and trust as the fundamental basis for doing business with consumers, customers, partners, suppliers, and each other. I talked about how all P&G-ers were owners of our company and leaders of their respective businesses. And I talked about the spirit of P&G, about P&G's passion for winning with those who matter most—consumers—and against our very best competitors.

I explicitly placed the consumer at the center of it all. I prioritized the consumer ahead of all other stakeholders, including customers, shareholders, and employees. I started with consumers, because the purpose of a business is to create consumers and to serve them better than anyone else can. No consumers, no business. I said P&G had to win the consumer value equation and the first two consumer moments of truth. I talked about retail customers and suppliers as partners in serving consumers better. I spoke of employees as the company's primary assets. I said that if P&G served more consumers better, if it innovated with its brands and products, its business models and work systems, and if we worked together more productively, then the company would grow and prosper and continue to be a preferred place of employment. Finally, I positioned our share price as a reflection of our ability to profitably serve more consumers better.

I really tried to distill things down as a way to get the choices understood. There's no doubt in my mind that clarity makes a difference. Clear and simple, easily translatable choices were crucial to get 135,000 P&G-ers in ninety countries operating with excellence every day.

Chapter Seven

Think Through Strategy

To this point, we have framed the five questions in the strategic choice cascade (what is your winning aspiration, where will you play, how will you win, what capabilities will you use, and what management systems will you employ?) and argued that all five must be answered, coordinated, and integrated to craft a powerful strategy and lasting competitive advantage. But how and where do you start? And how do you generate and choose between possibilities at each stage? For any company, there are many possible strategic choices that could be selected, an almost infinite amount of data that could be crunched, and a wide array of strategic tools that might be brought to bear on the problem. It can be overwhelming, even paralyzing. The bad news is that there is no simple algorithm for choice. The good news is that there is a framework that can give you a place to start.

As you begin articulating your strategic choice cascade, the obvious place to start is at the top. We've argued that it is essential to define a winning aspiration up front, and it does make sense to begin thinking about strategy by defining the purpose of your enterprise; without having an initial definition of winning, it is difficult to assess the value of any subsequent choice. You need a winning aspiration against which you can weigh different choices. But remember that strategy is an iterative process, and you'll need to return to refine your winning aspiration in the context of the subsequent choices. So, rather than dwell on crafting the perfect definition of winning, sketch a prototype, with the understanding that you will return to it later with the rest of the cascade in mind. Then consider the real work of strategy as beginning with where to play and how to win—the very heart of strategy. These are the choices that actually define what you will do, and where you will do it, so as to generate competitive advantage.

To define where to play and how to win, you'll need to understand and reflect on your context. To do so, you have scores of tools at your disposal—from simple analyses like SWOT (strengths, weaknesses, opportunities, and threats) to purpose-built tools like the Boston Consulting Group growth matrix and General Electric–McKinsey nine-box matrix to detailed frameworks based on particular strategic theories (the VRIN model, which assesses the degree to which the organization possesses capabilities that are valuable, rare, inimitable, and non-substitutable, and which emerged from the resource-based view of the firm). Each of these tools, frameworks, and philosophies has its most helpful uses, but none considers the full strategic landscape. Alone, none can help you decide where to play and how to win. Together, they produce a potentially unfocused and overwhelming mass of data and analysis. Instead of picking and choosing among these tools, companies need to develop a more directed approach that can be applied to make where-to-play and how-to-win choices across contexts.

Ultimately, there are four dimensions you need to think about to choose where to play and how to win:

1. *The industry.* What is the structure of your industry and the attractiveness of its segments?

2. *Customers.* What do your channel and end customers value?

3. *Relative position.* How does your company fare, and how could it fare, relative to the competition?

4. *Competition.* What will your competition do in reaction to your chosen course of action?

These four dimensions can be understood through a framework we call the *strategy logic flow*, which poses seven questions across the four dimensions (figure 7-1). The strategy logic flow spurs a thoughtful analysis of your company's current reality, context, challenges, and opportunities and leads to the development of multiple possible where-to-play and how-to-win choices.

The flow runs from left to right as a framing mechanism and a rough order of operations—though as with pretty much everything to do with strategy, a lot of iterative back-and-forth is required. The flow of the logic runs from industry to customers to relative position to competitive reaction. It is in considering all of these together that strategic choices emerge, but different dimensions will be more or less important in different contexts.

FIGURE 7-1

The strategy logic flow

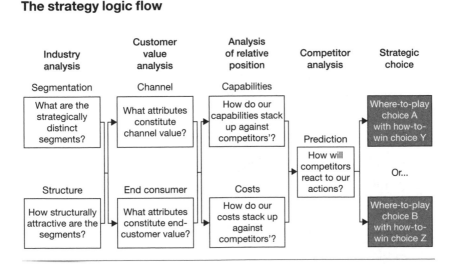

Industry Analysis

The first component of the strategy logic flow is industry analysis. To determine where to play, you must assess the industry landscape. You must ask, what might be the distinct segments of the industry in question (geographically, by consumer preference, by distribution channel, etc.)? Which segmentation scheme makes the most sense for the given industry today, and what might make sense in the future? And what is the relative attractiveness of those segments, now and in the future?

Segmentation

Industry segments are distinctive subsets of the larger industry along lines such as geography, product or service type, channel, customer or consumer needs, and so on. Mapping industry segments is rarely straightforward; it takes work, reflection, and, often, the willingness to explore beyond the current or obvious segments to segments that do not currently exist. In many cases, the accepted, traditional industry maps are imperfect. Like the old maps of a flat world that showed edges you could sail off, industry maps have limitations; only by exploring the edges of those maps can you see things differently.

In oral care at P&G, for instance, for many years the team thought about the industry in terms of products (brushes, pastes, and rinses) and consumer benefits (a huge segment devoted to cavity prevention and small segments devoted to appearance and to sensitive teeth). Crest was squarely in the huge and attractive cavity-prevention segment and winning big in the United States; it was number one in the industry for more than thirty years using this conceptualization of the industry structure. But the structure began to change in the 1990s. Cavity prevention became a generic benefit, one that every toothpaste brand could claim equally; this meant that other benefits would become increasingly important. On the strength of this insight, Colgate-Palmolive invented a new segment—based on a broader, "healthy mouth" consumer need—launching Colgate Total (which could fight cavities while also targeting tartar, plaque, bad breath, and gingivitis). Colgate Total came on the market in 1997 and within a year took over leading market share in toothpaste. It was a tactic P&G had employed many times over the years, inventing whole new segments with products like disposable diapers and anti-dandruff shampoo. Yet Colgate Total caught Crest flat-footed.

Hewing too close to a once highly successful map of the industry, Crest had been passed by an insurgent rival and was foundering. So the oral-care team, led by Mike Kehoe, the US manager of the oral-care category, undertook a fundamental rethink of the industry structure. The team started to consider oral care more broadly, in terms of a full regimen for the mouth and teeth rather than discrete products for a single job to be done. P&G launched Crest Whitestrips, SpinBrush Pro, oral rinse, and dental floss, broadening the Crest name from toothpaste to oral care. P&G began to embrace consumer needs more holistically to pursue several new segments, targeting those who care most about health, but also those who want whitening and even different product flavors. The company introduced Crest Pro-Health, Crest Vivid White, and a set of sensory Crest Expressions offerings, with flavors like cinnamon and vanilla. It took a decade, but Crest was able to reframe the business from toothpaste to oral care, to understand consumer preferences and unmet needs, and to broaden the product line in light of a richer understanding of industry segments.

Attractiveness

Once you have articulated existing and new segments, you must understand the structural attractiveness of the different segments. Other things being equal, a firm would want to play in segments that have higher profit potential based on their structural

FIGURE 7-2

Porter's five forces

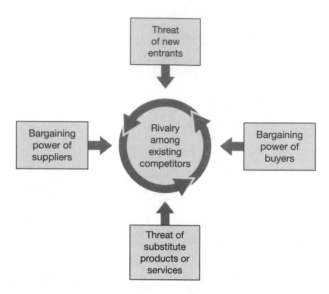

Source: Reprinted with permission from *On Competition*, by Michael E. Porter, Harvard Business School Press, 2008.

characteristics. To understand structural attractiveness, we can turn to Mike Porter's seminal five-forces analysis and ask about the bargaining power of suppliers, the bargaining power of buyers, the degree of rivalry, the threat of new entrants, and the threat of substitutes (figure 7-2). Porter's framework is a very useful aid to understanding the profit potential of markets and segments.

The five forces can be divided into two axes. The vertical axis—threat from new entrants and threat of substitute products—determines how much value is generated by the industry (and is therefore available to be split up among industry players). If it is very difficult for new players to enter the industry and there are no substitutes to the industry's product or services to which buyers can turn, then the industry will generate high value. This is why the pharmaceutical industry was so profitable through the 1980s and 1990s; it took enormous capital and expertise to get into the business and the buyers generally had little choice but to pay up for the products, which had no substitutes. Contrast this to the airline industry. There, whenever profitability spiked, a slew of new competitors entered. Or, compare it to steel, where everything from plastic to aluminum to ceramics to titanium can be a substitute.

The horizontal axis determines which entity will capture the industry value—suppliers, producers, or buyers. If the suppliers are larger and more powerful than the producers, the suppliers will appropriate more of the value (think Microsoft and Intel in the PC business). If, on the other hand, the buyers are large and powerful, they will get a greater portion of the value (think Walmart versus the many small manufacturers whose products fill their shelves). The degree to which there is fierce rivalry affects which group captures value too. If rivalry between competitors is high, the dynamic will facilitate the appropriation of value by suppliers or buyers. A low degree of rivalry will protect profitability for the producers.

At P&G, the analysis of segment attractiveness was occasionally a decisive factor in setting the strategy. For Bounty, geographic segmentation, paired with an understanding of consumer preferences, demonstrated that the paper-towel business was only structurally attractive for P&G in North America, due to massive overcapacity and low willingness to pay in the rest of the world. The industry featured high rivalry, high buyer power, and plenty of substitutes. When assessing segment attractiveness for Crest, P&G came to realize that the health segment was not only the largest, but also the most structurally attractive. Health claims need to be backed by clinical trials, and few companies—really only P&G and Colgate-Palmolive—have the resources and experience to play that game on an ongoing basis. This kind of analysis—crunching the numbers on the size and appeal of different segments—is crucial to determining the range of attractive where-to-play choices.

In general, P&G worked to tilt the weight of its portfolio toward more structurally attractive businesses, looking for businesses whose suppliers had little power to raise input costs. In beauty, for instance, purchased inputs were relatively low in value, making the sector more attractive to P&G.

Industries with fewer rivals and with competitors that seek to serve different parts of the market with unique offerings are more attractive than those in which a number of competitors compete fiercely for the same consumers in the same way. P&G favored beauty and personal care, including feminine care, because these were industries with low capital cost in which highly fragmented rivals attempted to differentiate their products in unique ways. In family care, by contrast, the machines that produce paper tissues and towels represent hundreds of millions in capital costs and are only profitable when running near capacity. Consequently, to keep their machines running to capacity, industry players tend to cut prices whenever demand softens. This diminishes structural attractiveness.

Porter's five forces help define the fundamental attractiveness of a given industry and its individual segments. Understanding structural attractiveness allows individual managers to determine how to invest in various segments within their business. For instance, the fine-fragrances business was able to initially avoid the intense competition in women's fragrances by starting with Hugo Boss in the more structurally attractive men's fragrance segment. Men's fragrance was more attractive because it was a smaller part of the market and most big competitors overlooked it to focus on women's prestige fragrances. After the business found its footing in men's fragrances, fine fragrances could leverage P&G's strengths to make the women's fragrance segment more attractive.

Industry analysis also enables a company to migrate its portfolio toward more structurally attractive businesses and away from less attractive ones. An analysis of the declining attractiveness of the hard-surface cleaner segment, for instance, led the category team to sell off Spic 'n Span and Comet, allocating resources to create new segments with Febreze (fabric odor removal) and Swiffer (quick floor cleaning), both much more structurally attractive than the traditional hard-surface cleaner segment and more conducive to building competitive advantage.

Customer Value Analysis

Armed with a map of the playing field and an analysis of the structural attractiveness of the individual segments, the strategist can move to the second major category in this framework: an analysis of customer value. Regardless of whether a firm wishes to be a cost leader or a differentiator, it needs to understand precisely what customers (its own and its competitors' customers) value. This means understanding underlying needs, like recognizing, with Gain, that a sizable group of consumers cared deeply about the sensory experience of doing laundry, valuing the scent of the detergent in the box, in the wash, and in the drawer or closet. Only once this need was understood was it possible to position and differentiate Gain along this dimension.

The logic flow diagram indicates two levels of customers, which may or may not be the case for a given firm. In many businesses, as with P&G, there is a distribution channel between the end consumer and the company. Individuals don't buy Gain directly from P&G; retailers buy from P&G, and then those retailers sell to end consumers. So, given that P&G needs retailers to stock Gain, the company needs to offer a compelling value proposition to retailers, or the end consumer will never see the product. Wherever there is an intermediary channel between the firm and the end consumer, that intermediate customer and what it values must be understood. Wherever there is no intermediate customer or channel (like a retail bank, for example, which offers services directly to its consumers), a direct-to-consumer or solely business-to-business firm can eliminate the channel box from the diagram.

In customer value analysis, the company assesses what its channel customers and end consumers really want and need, and what value they derive from the firm's products and services relative to the costs they incur from buying and using the products or services. For P&G, that means considering both its retail customers (like Walmart, Kroger, and Walgreens) and the consumers who actually buy and use the products. These two groups have different, and sometimes contradictory, benefits and costs. It is essential to understand both types of customers to make sense of and shape the full value equation. Once the value equation is understood, options will naturally begin to emerge for where to play and how to win.

Channel

For channel customers, profit margin, the ability to drive traffic, trade terms, and delivery consistency all tend to play into the value equation, along with many other variables that depend on the nature of the business. An understanding of the channel customer value equation can help inform both the businesses you should be in and how you can win there.

Understanding the channel value equation was particularly helpful to repositioning in oral care for P&G. At one time, P&G's non-toothpaste oral-care products were not terribly appealing to the retailers. Inexpensive toothbrushes and largely undifferentiated rinses or flosses sold at lower volume than toothpastes did and at a lower margin—which meant that retailers were fairly ambivalent about them. Higher-end items, like electric toothbrushes, might have offered attractive margins but little in the way of volume; they sat for a long time on the shelves without turning or earning the retailers that high margin. Retailers wanted products that would increase the total amount spent on oral care per visit—in other words, a bal-ance of profit and volume, driven by greater engagement with the category overall. The answer was innovation—margin-boosting differentiation on floss (through Teflon technology that would enable the floss to easily slide between teeth without shredding) and category-expanding products like the Crest SpinBrush (an affordable power brush that represented a trade-up from manual brushes) and Crest Whitestrips (a totally new consumer proposition for at-home teeth whitening) that brought in entirely new spending.

The dynamics of channel value were also essential to the Olay choice to stay in mass retail rather than moving up to department stores. In department and specialty stores, the manufacturer staffs its own mini beauty store within a larger retail format. Such a struc-ture adds considerable complexity and lots of costs as the numer-ous cosmetics and skin-care competitors ratchet up the grandeur of their space and their level of staffing. Better to leverage existing retail relationships, the team decided, working with these retail-ers to create new value through an Olay premium-priced masstige positioning, which traded up current mass customers and attracted prestige customers from department and specialty stores. This strat-egy created more volume, profit, and margin for the mass retailers.

Understanding customer value requires deep engagement. The traditional approach of checking in with salespeople occasionally to see what retailers are thinking and doing is no longer enough. A much higher level of sophistication—and real commitment—is required. Almost twenty years ago, P&G began integrating staff from marketing, manufacturing, logistics, finance, IT, and human resources into customer teams in customer business development (P&G's sales function). These teams were colocated near P&G's largest customers, like Walmart, Target, and Tesco. The post-1999 focus on core customers—those who accounted for an overwhelm-ing share of P&G sales and profits—helped redefine the role of these multifunctional customer teams. Their job was to understand their customer so well that they could work collaboratively to develop mutual business goals, joint value creation strategies, and shared action plans to win. The focus of the combined customer and P&G team was always on the *how*—whether it was identifying how to take costs out of the supply chain or how to better serve a customer's shoppers to drive traffic and sales. This shared focus has resulted in joint value creation—creating strategic payoffs both for the customer and for P&G.

End Consumers

Understanding end consumers is a challenging thing, because you can't simply ask what they want, need, and value. Recall Henry Ford's famous quip that if, at the dawn of the automotive industry, he'd asked consumers what they wanted, they would have said, "A faster horse." To understand the consumer value equation, you must truly get to know your consumers—to engage with them beyond the quantitative survey, through deeper, more personal forms of research—watching them shop, listening to their stories, visiting them at home to observe how they use and evaluate your products. Only through this kind of deep user understanding can you hope to generate insights about where to play and how to win.

So it was with baby diapers. By focusing entirely on technology (making the diaper more and more absorbent), the category had lost touch with mom. When it reengaged with her, the diaper team found out that while absorbency was important, so too were a soft, cloth-like feel, easy-to-use tabs, a snug but comfortable waist, and even a fun design. It turned out that mothers valued familiar characters, like the Sesame Street gang, over the nondescript cartoon bears P&G had been using. Understanding mothers better also led the business to change how it "sized" the diapers, moving from a weight-based designation (e.g., for fifteen- to twenty-pound babies) to life stage (like Swaddlers and Cruisers) that matched with how mom thought about her baby.

To better understand the end consumer, P&G spent much of the decade of the 2000s retooling the Market Research Department, which had historically focused on doing highly quantitative consumer research (to choose between product, packaging, and marketing options and to forecast volume for product launches and initiatives), into Consumer and Market Knowledge (CMK), a group capable of employing both quantitative and qualitative research approaches, together with world-leading technologies in decision modeling, such as agent-based modeling, to create a robust picture of markets, segments, and consumers. Part of CMK's advance in consumer understanding came by way of insights from the world of design. There, ethnographic study of what consumers actually do—rather than what they say they do—is an important step to gaining a deep and holistic understanding of users. In part through the design initiative headed by P&G's first ever vice president of design strategy and innovation, Claudia Kotchka, ethnographic research became an essential part of the P&G consumer understanding toolbox.

Often during the customer analysis stage, the industry thinking needs to be revisited. With more customer knowledge, the industry map can change. This certainly happened when oral care took an updated look at the dentifrice map and saw that the once-giant cavity-protection segment wasn't so giant anymore. It needed to be both resized (the pure "all I think about is cavity protection" segment was tiny) and recast (to capture a holistic mouth-health segment).

Analysis of Relative Position

With an understanding of the industry and customers, the next step is to explore your own relative position on two levels: capabilities and costs.

Capabilities

In terms of relative capabilities, the question is, how do your capabilities stack up, and how could they stack up, against those of your competitors in meeting the identified needs of customers (both channel and end consumer)? In particular, could you configure your capabilities to enable your company to meet the needs of customers in a distinctively valuable way, underpinning a potential differentiation strategy? Or, at a minimum, could you configure your capabilities to enable the company to match competitors in meeting the needs of customers, underpinning a potential cost-leadership strategy? In other words, how could your capabilities be configured to translate to a measurable, sustainable competitive advantage?

As with each of the other elements in the logic flow, an assessment of relative capabilities proved decisive for a number of strategic choices at P&G. For instance, it led the company to exit several profitable businesses, like pharmaceuticals, which required a number of capabilities that did not fit well within the P&G structure. Pharmaceuticals require a long, complex clinical trial and FDA-approval process; they are largely sold directly to doctors and pharmacies, with little or no ability to influence the end consumer; for many of the products, there was no long-term usage opportunity, which made it hard to use P&G brand-building capabilities to build a sustainable tie with consumers; and there was little crossover between P&G core technologies and the technologies needed to innovate in pharmaceuticals. So, P&G exited the industry, after much debate and soul-searching.

Costs

The other half of an analysis of relative position relates to cost and the degree to which the organization can achieve approximate cost parity with competitors or distinctly lower costs than competitors.

These are the key questions to consider on this front: does the organization have a scale, branding, or product development advantage that enables it to deliver a superior value offering at the same cost as the cost incurred by competitors? Or, does it have a scale advantage, a learning-curve advantage, a proprietary process, or a technology that enables it to have a superior cost position? The answers to these questions start to put parameters around the myriad how-to-win options.

At P&G, costs have been a particularly crucial concern for highly price-sensitive industries and categories like fabric care, family care, and, of course, emerging markets, where incomes are much lower. As detailed elsewhere in this book, P&G needed to find new ways to deliver an affordable diaper, razor, or shampoo, customized to market conditions and matching the ability of consumers to pay. But relative cost was a concern for Olay as well. By staying in the mass channel, P&G could have a dramatically lower cost structure than its prestige competitors, which needed to invest massively in store fixtures and in-store personnel. The cost savings from keeping Olay in mass retail could be funneled into innovation and marketing to create competitive advantage. Finally, in GBS, costs have been a key factor in P&G's strategy, which has been to consolidate and outsource where possible, to enable cost savings to be invested in boosting core capabilities throughout the organization.

Competitive Analysis

Thinking through the first six boxes in figure 7-1 should produce a range of potential where-to-play and how-to-win choices. Before even thinking about deciding between these possibilities, you need to evaluate these potential places to play and ways to win for robustness against your current competitive strategies and anticipated competitor reaction. This is the fourth and final element of the logic flow. The question to address is this: is there some competitive response that could undermine or trump the where-to-play and how-to-win choices?

Inevitably, this is guesswork to some degree; you can't know for sure what a competitor will or won't do in the face of your actions. But forming a thoughtful hypothesis is important. It is far better to ask what your competitors will likely do before you proceed than to simply wait and see what happens. Only strategies that provide a sustainable advantage—or a significant lead in developing future advantages—are worth investing in. You don't want to design and build a strategy that a competitor can copy in a heartbeat, or one that will prove ineffective against a simple defensive maneuver on a competitor's part. A strategy that only works if competitors continue to do exactly what they are already doing is a dangerous strategy indeed.

An analysis of the competitive landscape and potential competitive reaction was particularly decisive in the Impress and ForceFlex technologies, the bags and wraps innovations that would eventually form the basis of P&G's joint venture with Glad. The family-care team was quite sure that P&G's entry into an already competitive space would cause an all-out war, one in which P&G might not prevail, even with a superior technology. So the team knew it needed to find another way to play to win. The analysis of anticipated competitive response was the spur to create a new and better strategy for commercializing the technologies.

Competitive reaction was also a crucial consideration in P&G's decision to launch a new dish detergent in Japan in the 1990s. At the time, the market was dominated by two massive players: Kao and Lion. Both sold dish soap in bottles that were quite sizable because the soap was diluted with lots of water. There was little differentiation between the products, other than name and fragrance.

Bob McDonald, then vice president of laundry and cleaning products in Asia (and soon to be president of Japan operations), and
his team saw an opportunity to launch Joy, using the proprietary
grease-fighting technology from P&G's successful US Dawn brand.
The product would be sold in a highly concentrated form, in a bottle one-quarter the size of competitive offerings.

Joy looked to be a good fit with consumer values (a better
grease-fighting technology was the answer to a genuine consumer
need), and the team believed it could get retailers excited about selling more bottles with less shelf space and a healthy price premium.
But how would the entrenched and powerful competitors react?
The team modeled the possible reactions and determined that if the
competitors stayed with their existing diluted format, Joy could win
handily. If the competitors chose to launch a concentrated version,
but continued to produce diluted as well, Joy would still win, as
the competition would face considerably higher costs and be challenged by a split focus. The only real danger was if the competitors
dropped their diluted versions and threw everything behind new,
concentrated detergents. If they did, Joy would have little chance
with a similar product going against established local competitors.

The team had to make its best guess about the competitors'
likely course of action. Kao and Lion were large, traditional firms
with a great deal invested in their current approach, especially
given that the vast majority of their category profit came from these
diluted formulas. The team believed that at worst, the competitors
would move to producing both dilute and concentrate. This would
give Joy time to gain a foothold. The competitors indeed chose to
defend their existing dilute product lines while also launching a
concentrated version—which gave Joy the opportunity to create a
sizable new segment and take most of it. By 1997, Joy had captured
30 percent of the total dish detergent market and was the number
one dish brand in the country.

A Framework for Strategy

To make good choices, you need to make sense of the complexity of your environment. The strategy logic flow can point you to the key areas of analysis necessary to generate sustainable competitive advantage. First, look to understand the industry in which you play (or will play), its distinct segments and their relative attractiveness. Without this step, it is all too easy to assume that your map of the world is the only possible map, that the world is unchanging, and that no better possibilities exist. Next, turn to customers. What do channel and end consumers truly want, need, and value—and how do those needs fit with your current or potential offerings? To answer this question, you will have to dig deep—engaging in joint value creation with channel partners and seeking a new understanding of end consumers. After customers, the lens turns inward: what are your capabilities and costs relative to the competition? Can you be a differentiator or a cost leader? If not, you will need to rethink your choices. Finally, consider competition; what will your competitors do in the face of your actions? Throughout the thinking process, be open to recasting previous analyses in light of what you learn in a subsequent box. The basic direction of the process is from left to right, but it also has interdependencies that require a more flexible path through it.

Working through the framework takes both patience and imagination. It also takes teamwork. Any new strategy is created in a social context—it isn't devised by an individual sitting alone in an office, thinking his or her way through a complex situation. Rather, strategy requires a diverse team with the various members bringing their distinct perspectives to bear on the problem. A process for working collaboratively on strategy is essential, because all companies are social entities, made up of a diverse network of individuals with different agendas and ideas. Those people need to think, communicate, decide, and take action together, in order to accomplish anything meaningful. The logic flow, as we have seen, is a tool that simplifies thinking about strategy by laying out its foundational analytical components and providing a consistent way to put the pieces together. But the framework alone isn't enough to ensure that sound strategic choices are made within a company. You also need a process to facilitate making choices together. This is the subject of the next chapter.

STRATEGY LOGIC FLOW DOS AND DON'TS

- ✓ Do explore all four critical dimensions of strategy choice: industry, customers, relative position, and competition.

- ✓ Do look beyond your current understanding of the industry, pushing to generate new ways of segmenting the market.

- ✓ Don't accept that entire industries are or must be unattractive; explore the drivers of different dynamics in different segments, and ask how the game could be changed.

- ✓ Do consider both channel and end consumer value equations; if only one of these constituents is happy, your strategy is a fragile one. A winning strategy is a win-win-win; it creates value for consumers, customers, and the company.

- ✓ Don't expect either the channel or the end consumers to tell you what constitutes value; that is your job to figure out.

- ✓ Don't be blasé about your relative capabilities or costs; compare them with those of your best competition, and really push to understand how you can win against them.

- ✓ Do explore a range of possible competitive reactions to your choices, and ask under what conditions competitors could block you from winning.

THE LONG ROAD TO THE LOGIC FLOW

by Roger L. Martin

Looking back on it, I see that the journey toward the strategy logic flow was long and winding. One wouldn't have thought so, with Michael Porter providing the foundational intellectual property with his smash hit 1980 book *Competitive Strategy* and its 1985 follow-up *Competitive Advantage*. Just read the book, and do strategy! Sadly, it wasn't quite that simple for me.

In my early Monitor days, it was striking how many clients simply asked for individual analyses that they'd read about in Porter's book: "Do a five-forces analysis for us; do a competitor analysis for us." So we did. It was considerably tougher when a client asked us to devise a better strategy for the company. But my Monitor colleagues and I were bright and energetic and steeped in Porter's tools, so we could always go back to the office, get to thinking, and pull something good out of the proverbial black box. The real trick, though, was when clients asked us to teach them how to do strategy, to show them how to get from an unsatisfactory strategy to a great one themselves. That was something much, much harder to do.

In 1987, Eaton Corporation hired us to do just that: work with its various divisions to teach them how to create great strategies. I was dispatched to Battle Creek, Michigan, to work with their truck axle business. As I went through the first training session, I became painfully aware that I was teaching the Eaton managers a series of analytical tools related to strategy, rather than a holistic process for creating strategy. I found myself asking, how exactly does customer analysis relate to competitor analysis to relative cost analysis to five-forces analysis?

Since my clients were getting a fire-hose blast of new content, they seemed oblivious to the gap in the material. But I remember going back to my hotel room one night and drawing a diagram that attempted to fit the pieces together. Where do you start? How does one analysis lead to the next?

Not long after that first attempt to put the analytical tools into a single robust framework, I was asked to work on the applied strategic management (ASM) program for P&G, when CEO John Smale asked Monitor to create a program that taught P&G category-management teams the strategy tools that we used. Colleagues Mark Fuller, Bob Lurie, and I were responsible for creating a three-day program and then teaching it to category teams in the four global regions. At first, I focused on advancing the state of the art by sequencing the teaching of the various tools. Eaton Corporation had taught me that it was hard to have a useful or intelligent discussion of capabilities analysis before understanding what customers actually want, so we taught customer analysis before capabilities analysis. But since all customers aren't the same, we had to teach industry analysis and segmentation before customer analysis—oops, that was tricky, because we traditionally taught segmentation as part of customer analysis. Competitor analysis was equally tricky. I put it at the end, because I felt that competitive *reaction* was critically important. But of course, some things about competitors had to be understood earlier on (to analyze relative capabilities, for instance).

While it was still not a robust process for actually doing strategy, ASM represented a significant advance over my work at Eaton Corporation. The analytical tools were taught in a significantly more organized fashion, for instance. Moreover, two very good things

came out of ASM. First, because P&G has such talented managers, a number of them figured out how to put the pieces together
into a true process for doing strategy. Almost a decade later, one
P&G executive pulled out of his top desk drawer a single lami-
nated sheet with his distillation of the ASM into a strategy process, one that he used regularly to do strategy. It was a thing of
beauty! Others within P&G also used ASM principles routinely to
develop their strategies, creating the foundation of a true strategy practice at P&G. Second, teaching ASM over and over (there
were about twenty categories per region to teach across four
regions) helped me better understand the real strategy questions these managers faced and how the tools did or did not
help them think about those challenges. I came to understand
how bundling a number of aspects into a single analytical tool—
for example, grouping under *competitor analysis* the prediction of
competitor reaction, the analysis of competitor cost structure,
and the analysis of competitor capabilities—made it difficult for
managers to apply the analysis productively.

Our work on the ASM and, subsequently, P&G's principles of
strategic management program, continued through 1989 and
set the stage for my work at Weston Foods in 1990. A multi-
billion-dollar subsidiary of George Weston Limited, Weston Foods
had a new CEO, David Beatty, and executive vice president, Jim
Fisher, both of whom were exceedingly bright and experienced
former McKinsey consultants. A highly diversified business run
mainly by very traditional food-industry business unit presidents,
Weston Foods had rarely done any strategy at all. Planning was
primarily a financial budgeting process. To improve Weston
Foods' middling performance, Beatty and Fisher wanted to install

modern strategic planning processes and hired me to help them do so. The centerpiece of the work was to be an off-site meeting to teach the business unit presidents and finance heads. At this meeting, they would be taught a strategy framework and begin to frame their strategic planning challenges.

I freely admit to struggling mightily before that meeting to put onto paper the things that I had learned from Eaton, P&G, and elsewhere. A couple days before the off-site meeting, I finally came to a format for characterizing the thinking process of strategy—a framework that became the logic flow. I reduced the challenge to the key questions that needed to be answered to formulate a where-to-play and how-to-win choice. There were seven questions arrayed under four broad analytical categories and organized into a flow from industry to customer to relative position to competitor. It wasn't entirely linear and unidirectional in practice, of course—there are all sorts of feedback loops and subroutines—but this new structure provided a straightforward organization of the logical flow for thinking through strategy choices.

Most importantly, it worked. The teams at Weston Foods, with no strategy experience, were able to work through a process and dramatically raise the quality of the strategy dialogue. I walked away pleased and inspired. The logic flow, a way of thinking about strategy, would become the foundation of my strategy consulting practice for the next decade and beyond.

Chapter Eight

Shorten Your Odds

In strategy, there are no absolute answers or sure things, and nothing lasts forever. Having a clear definition of winning, a robust analytical framework such as the logic flow, and a thoughtful review process can help organize thinking and improve analysis, but even still, a successful outcome is not guaranteed. In the end, building a strategy isn't about achieving perfection; it's about shortening your odds.

Generating Buy-In: The Traditional Approach

In a typical strategy process, participants seek to find the single right answer, build unassailable arguments to support it, and sell it to the rest of the organization (figure 8-1). At the beginning, an internal project team or an external consultant, or both, will set out to rigorously analyze everything they can to ferret out answers about the world—what consumers want, the competitive dynamics of the industry, and so on. Or perhaps the team already has a view as to what the right answer will be, so it conducts analyses that are designed to confirm the hypothesis. Either way, a dive into the data is the starting point.

At some point, through the cloud of data, a few plausible strategic options emerge. Because there is intense pressure to be practical, creativity is tacitly discouraged throughout the option-generation process. The team sees it as its job to ensure that all of the options will ultimately be actionable. The implication is that unexpected (even wild) strategic options and creative ideas will slow down the process and add no value—and might become dangerous if momentum is built behind them. So there is a drive to expected, straightforward options that stay relatively close to home. Then, the options are typically assessed using a single metric: the financial plausibility test. A high net present value or internal rate of return helpfully buttresses the claim that a particular option is the best choice.

At this stage, arguments often ensue as to which truly is the superior option, with each side dipping into the vast body of analysis for proof or tweaking the assumptions behind the financial metric. To create a consensus, the team makes a series of compromises to bring key managers on-side. The compromise option is then taken to senior management (or the board of directors), where it is aggressively sold as the right answer. With perhaps a little more compromising to get senior managers on board, the choice is given final approval and the strategy is rolled out to the organization.

The problems with this traditional approach are numerous. First, it is expensive and time-consuming to analyze everything up front. The analysis itself tends to be scattershot and superficial, because there is so much material to cover. Plus, because so many different analyses are being conducted, they are often done independently of one another, making it difficult to see the whole picture at any point. Hard feelings tend to emerge as individuals advocate for one choice or another and feel marginalized if their

FIGURE 8-1

Generating buy-in

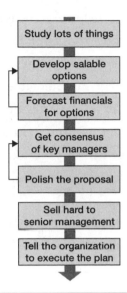

option doesn't make the cut. Since the goal is for everyone to buy in, weak compromises are made instead of real, hard choices. Creativity is discouraged; the pressure to converge on an answer on the basis of existing data eliminates the possibilities that are off the mainstream path. The buy-in process is long and tedious, yet it often results in only the appearance of concurrence, followed by foot-dragging by those who never truly bought in. And senior management is engaged only at the end of the process, after the strategy is buttoned up, which means that these leaders' experience, insights, and ideas are barely taken into account (if at all). In all, it is a painful and unproductive process that produces few powerful choices. No wonder managers have little enthusiasm for the strategy process.

Asking the Right Question

Asking a single question can change everything: what would have to be true? This question helpfully focuses the analysis on the things that matter. It creates room for inquiry into ideas, rather than advocacy of positions. It encourages a broader consideration of more options, particularly unpredictable ones. It provides room to explore ideas before the team settles on a final answer. It dramatically reduces intrateam tension and conflict, during decision making and afterward. It turns unproductive conflict into healthy tension focused on finding the best strategic approach. And it leads to clear strategic choices at the end.

We all ultimately want to find the strategy that is best for our business. Rather than asking individuals to find that answer for themselves and then fight it out, this approach enables the team to uncover the strongest option together. A standard process is characterized by arguments about *what is true.* By turning instead to exploring *what would have to be true*, teams go from battling one another to working together to explore ideas. Rather than attempting to bury real disagreements, this approach surfaces differences and resolves them, resulting in more-robust strategies and stronger commitment to them.

The process for exploring what would have to be true has seven specific steps, as seen in figure 8-2. It begins with framing the fundamental choice, articulating at least two different ways forward for the organization (or category, function, brand, product, etc.), on the basis of your winning aspiration. Then, the team works to brainstorm a wider variety of possible strategic choices, different where-to-play and how-to-win choice combinations that could result in winning. These strategic possibilities are then each considered in turn by asking what would have to be true for this possibility to be a potentially winning choice. (Or, flipped around, by asking, under what conditions could we win with this possibility?)

FIGURE 8-2

Reverse-engineering strategic options

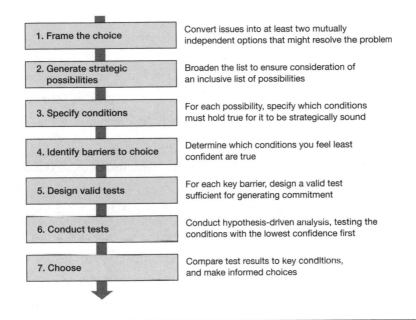

1. Frame the choice	Convert issues into at least two mutually independent options that might resolve the problem
2. Generate strategic possibilities	Broaden the list to ensure consideration of an inclusive list of possibilities
3. Specify conditions	For each possibility, specify which conditions must hold true for it to be strategically sound
4. Identify barriers to choice	Determine which conditions you feel least confident are true
5. Design valid tests	For each key barrier, design a valid test sufficient for generating commitment
6. Conduct tests	Conduct hypothesis-driven analysis, testing the conditions with the lowest confidence first
7. Choose	Compare test results to key conditions, and make informed choices

The answers—the things that would have to be true—are the conditions under which the group would choose to move ahead with a particular possibility. At this stage, there is no discussion of whether the conditions are likely to hold, just an understanding that if they did hold, this possibility would be a great choice.

Next, the group reflects on the set of conditions and asks which of those conditions seem the least likely to hold. These least-likely-to-be-true conditions are the barriers to selecting a given option; until the group has some confidence as to whether these conditions hold, it is impossible to move ahead with a possibility. So, the team must design and conduct tests of those barriers. As each possibility is assessed in this way, a clear picture emerges as to which conditions actually hold and which choice is the most robust. The best strategic choice gradually becomes clear.

This is the process in abstract form. Now, let's dive into more detail on each stage, returning to our first example, Olay, as the illustration.

1. Frame the Choice

As a general rule, an issue—for example, declining sales or technology change in the industry—can't be resolved until it is framed as a choice. Until a real choice (e.g., should the company go in this direction or that one?) is articulated, team members can't understand cognitively or feel emotionally the consequences of the different ways to resolve the issue. A team could talk endlessly about declining sales, making no progress toward solving the problem. But crystallizing the issue by clearly framing the choices for resolving it makes the issue immediately real and meaningful. For example, a team might ask, should it invest to reinvigorate the product line, cut costs through head-count reductions, or exit the business entirely? Articulating options provides a gut check. The team can ask, how do those choices feel, and more importantly, what would it need to know to decide on the best choice?

To frame the choice, explicitly ask, what are the different ways of resolving this problem? Work to generate several options that stand in opposition to one another (i.e., such that you could not easily pursue the different remedies at the same time). Until you have identified a minimum of two mutually exclusive options to resolve the issue, the choice is not truly framed. This stage, framing the choice, is the proverbial crossing of the Rubicon; it makes the stakes clear and the consequences apparent and motivates the team to move ahead with finding the best answer it can.

With Olay, framing the choice was crucial. It made the stakes clear immediately. Rather than agonizing endlessly about what to do with a fading brand, the team framed the choice and provided an impetus to action. The team laid out two possibilities: it could attempt to transform Oil of Olay into a worthy competitor to brands like Lancôme and La Prairie, or it could spend billions of dollars to buy a major existing skin-care brand to compete instead.

2. Generate Strategic Possibilities

Framing the issue as a choice identifies a preliminary set of options for resolving the problem; the next task is to broaden the list of possibilities. The objective in this step is to be inclusive rather than restrictive of the number and diversity of possibilities on the table. Here is the opportunity to encourage creative and more-unexpected strategies. In this context, a possibility should be expressed as a narrative or scenario, a happy story that describes a positive outcome. That is why we like to call them possibilities rather than options. Characterizing the possibilities as stories helps ensure that they are not seen negatively as unsubstantiated opinions. No one is yet arguing for a possibility; you and your colleagues are simply envisioning a world in which that story makes good sense.

Possibilities should be welcomed at this stage, not thoroughly vetted for inclusion. Suggested possibilities should never be trivialized or dismissed, lest that discourage the inclusion of more out-of-the-box ideas in the consideration set. Within the group, there must be a fundamental commitment to openness, such that if any member of the group feels that a given possibility is worth exploring, it should automatically be included in the choice set. Culling a possibility about which a particular individual feels strongly may well cause that individual to withdraw, perhaps for the rest of the process. So inclusion, rather than exclusion, is the rule at this stage.

Inevitably, as the creative possibilities pile up, group members may begin to feel uncomfortable. Just the act of considering some choices may feel downright seditious. But be assured that this is only the beginning of a longer process. Every choice will have its logic laid out in precisely the same manner and will be held to the highest standards of assessment. Subsequent steps of the process will weed out possibilities appropriately, so it is unnecessary (and unhelpful) to do so at this stage.

The possibilities generated may be related to the options already identified, as either amplifications or nuances. Oil of Olay possibilities that derived from the initial options included growing Oil of Olay within its existing pricing tier or taking it upmarket, buying Nivea, or purchasing Clinique. The possibilities can also expand further beyond the original two options. For P&G's beauty business, ideas included extending its successful color cosmetics brand, Cover Girl, into skin care and building a global brand from that platform.

In the end, the P&G beauty team focused on five where-to-play and how-to-win possibilities for skin care. One was to largely give up on Oil of Olay and to acquire a major global skin-care brand. A second was to keep Oil of Olay positioned as an entry-priced, mass-market brand, strengthening its appeal to current consumers by leveraging R&D capabilities to improve wrinkle-fighting performance. A third was to take Oil of Olay up-market into the prestige distribution channel as an upscale brand. A fourth was to reinvent Olay totally—as a prestige-like brand that appealed more broadly to younger women (age thirty-five to fifty), but sold in the traditional mass channels with retail partners that would be willing to create a masstige experience with a special display section in the store. A fifth was to extend the Cover Girl brand from cosmetics into skin care.

3. Specify Conditions

Once a diverse set of possibilities is established, the team then needs to reverse engineer the logic of each possibility. That is, it needs to specify what must be true for the possibility to be a terrific choice. Notice, this step is decidedly not for arguing about what is true, but rather for laying out the logic of what would have to be true for the group to collectively commit to a choice.

The difference between the two approaches cannot be overstated. In a standard strategy discussion, skeptics attack ideas as vigorously as possible to knock options out of contention, and defenders parry the arguments to protect pet options. Tempers rise, statements get more extreme, and relationships are strained. Meanwhile, little new or helpful information emerges. If instead the dialogue is about what would have to be true, then the skeptic can say, "For me to be confident in this possibility, we would have to know that consumers would respond in the following way." This is a very different sort of statement than "That option will never work! Consumers hate that approach." Rather than a blanket denunciation of a possibility, skeptics in the reverse-engineering process must specify the exact source of their skepticism. This frame helps the possibility's proponents understand the reservations and creates a standard of proof to address them.

This process is a form of reverse engineering because the starting point is the (tentative) assumption that the conclusion is valid—namely, that this is a great possibility. The team then works to understand the conditions under which that assumption is correct. It works backward to declare the various conditions that would have to hold for this to be a great possibility. Figure 8-3 shows the logic flow of this reverse-engineering exercise. In each of the seven boxes, you can list *what would have to be true* along that dimension for the option in question to be valid.

At this reverse-engineering stage, there is absolutely no interest in opinions as to whether the conditions pertaining to a given possibility are true. In fact, expressing such opinions is counterproductive. The only interest is in ferreting out what would have to be true for every member of the group to feel intellectually and emotionally committed to the possibility under consideration.

FIGURE 8-3

Laying out the conditions

To pursue this possibility, what would have to be true?

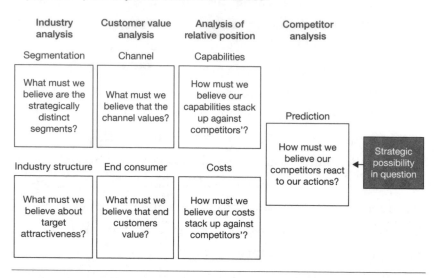

Reservations are important and must be taken into consideration, but only in the form of conditions that would have to be true (and not as explicit criticism of the validity of the possibility).

It is important that every individual's conditions are given equal consideration, to ensure that no one fails to engage, out of fear or embarrassment. But it is equally important that options are reverse engineered by the group, not the individual who first suggested the possibility. There is no ownership of possibilities by individuals, lest the process derail. To help separate individuals from ideas, you could have an outside facilitator to guide the team through the process, drawing out contributions from quieter voices and attempting to capture all possibilities. Having at least one person in the room with an investment in the process but no strong view about the outcome can be extremely helpful. The reverse-engineering chart for Olay would look something like the one in figure 8-4, with conditions spanning all seven boxes.

FIGURE 8-4

The Olay masstige option

The option under consideration was to reposition Olay for a younger demographic, with the promise to "fight the seven signs of aging." It would involve partnering with retailers to create a masstige segment—consumers willing to buy a prestige-like product in mass channels. P&G determined that for this option to succeed, these conditions would have to exist or be created:

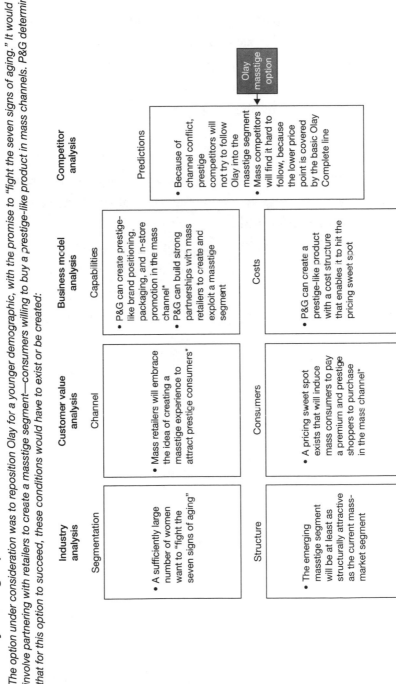

* Barrier conditions—the ones P&G thought least likely would hold true.

Under industry analysis, to proceed with building a masstige segment for Olay, there would have to be a large segment of women who care about multiple signs of aging, and these women would have to respond to a compelling brand and product offering on this front. The new masstige segment would have to be at least as structurally attractive as Oil of Olay's existing mass segment in terms of buyer power, supplier power, threat of new entrants, substitutes, and competitive rivalry.

In terms of the customer value analysis, the mass channel would have to embrace the masstige concept and be willing to work with P&G to create the kind of in-store experience that would support the new segment and reinforce the Olay brand. On the consumer side, P&G would have to be able to find a winning price that would attract both mass and prestige consumers. To work, masstige offerings would need to trade up mass consumers to more-expensive products and drive prestige shoppers to purchase in a new channel.

On analysis of relative position, a number of conditions related to capabilities in product development, retail partnerships, and brand building would have to be true. In the cost box, P&G would have to be able to create a prestige-like, superior product at a cost that would enable a pricing structure just below the prestige brands.

Finally, what would have to be true about the competitive reaction? Prestige competitors, bound tightly to their preferred and well-known channels, would have to refrain from shifting to the mass channel. Also, mass competitors would have to be incapable of credibly creating competitive products from a technology and branding point of view, because of the importance of low prices to their positioning and the limits of their capabilities relative to P&G's.

Once a full set of conditions is articulated, the list can be pared back by the group. To do so, ask about each condition: if all the other conditions were found to hold but this one didn't, would that eliminate this possibility? This helps distinguish between the nice-to-have conditions and the must-have conditions. Typically during the generation of conditions, a number of the former are mixed in with the latter. One condition might be, for instance, that retailers would have to be able to earn higher margins on this product than on current ones. That would certainly be nice. But if retailers could derive value in other ways (e.g., through incremental sales), the margins could be the same and the trade would still be supportive. Nice-to-have conditions need to be culled so that every condition is actually a binding one. The process of reverse engineering is complete only when each group member understands the logic of the possibility and can say, "Yes, if all of those conditions were true, this would be a great possibility. And if any single condition weren't true, this would not be a good possibility."

4. Identify Barriers to Choice

The fourth step in the process constitutes a 180-degree flip. The previous step stayed assiduously away from opinions on whether the conditions would hold true. This creates an environment that enables each team member to explore the logic behind the possibility and to codify and organize it. Now, and only now, you can cast a critical eye on the conditions your team has identified. The task is to assess which of the conditions your team believes are the least likely to hold true. In other words, now that you've specified what would have to be true for this possibility to be a great idea, which of those conditions worry the team the most and seem the least likely to be true? These conditions constitute the barriers that keep you and the team from choosing that possibility. Until you know if they are true or not, you can't move ahead.

In this step, it is extremely important to pay close attention to the group member who is the most skeptical that a condition will hold true; a skeptic can provide extremely valuable insurance against making a bad choice. So skeptical group members must be encouraged to raise, not suppress, concerns at this point in the process. Even if only one person has concerns about a given condition, it should remain on the list of key barriers. Otherwise, the skeptic would be within his or her rights to dismiss the final analysis. If the key concerns of the team members are drawn out and taken seriously, all can feel confident in the process and the outcomes.

When the P&G beauty team members reviewed the conditions for the Olay masstige possibility, they felt confident that six would hold: the potential consumer segment was big enough to be worth targeting, it was likely to be sufficiently structurally attractive, P&G was capable of building retailer partnerships (if retailers liked the idea), P&G could achieve the necessary cost structure to make the product profitable, prestige competitors would not copy the strategy, and mass competitors could not copy the strategy. However, three conditions were worrisome (in order from greatest concern to least): that mass channel consumers would accept a new, significantly higher starting price point; that mass channel retailers would be game to partner to create this new masstige segment; and that P&G could bring together prestige-like brand positioning, product, and packaging and in-store promotion elements in the mass retail channel.

5. Design Valid Tests

Once key barrier conditions are identified, they must be tested in ways the entire group will find compelling. A test may involve surveying a thousand consumers or speaking to only one supplier. It may entail crunching thousands of numbers or doing a purely qualitative assessment. In the case of Olay, the pricing condition was a significant barrier. So, P&G conducted a number of market tests for different price points ($12.99, $15.99, and $18.99, as discussed in chapter 1). But not all companies can afford full market tests; nor are pilots practical for every instance. In some cases, you need to be creative about tests, perhaps looking at analogous industries in which repositioning created loyal customers or failed to do so. P&G did this for competitive reaction—without actually inciting the feared reaction in the market, the team projected possible outcomes according to past reactions to determine what each competitor might do.

At this point, the critical issue is whether the decision-making group regards the test as valid. In this sense, the most skeptical member of the team is the most valuable. Typically, this person will have the highest standard of proof for any test, and building his or her commitment to the choice will be the most challenging. However, without his or her commitment, any consensus will inevitably be false. Hence, the most effective approach to overcoming barriers is to put the test design for each barrier condition in the hands of that condition's greatest skeptic. If that person is satisfied that a test is rigorous and that the standard of proof has been passed, then everybody else—who is by definition less skeptical—will also be satisfied that the test is legitimate and stringent.

The danger, of course, is that this approach will result in the skeptic's setting an unachievable standard to undermine the possibility. This could theoretically happen. However, empirically, it does not happen, for two reasons. First, people demonstrate extremes of skepticism largely because they don't feel heard. In a typical buy-in process, concerns are roadblocks to be pushed out of the way as quickly and thoroughly as possible. The reverse-engineering process, by contrast, makes sure that individuals with concerns feel heard and actually are heard. Second, there is the specter of mutually assured destruction. Though I may have serious doubts about possibility A, I quite like possibility B. You, on the other hand, have few doubts about possibility A, but serious barriers to choosing possibility B. I get to set the tests for the barrier conditions for possibility A, but I do so in the knowledge that you will get to set the tests for possibility B. If I set an unrealistically high bar for the tests for A, you will surely do the same for B. Being fair is the smartest approach to ensure the best outcome for the organization—something all participants both desire.

The ultimate goal is to design tests that will enable each member of the group to put hand on heart and commit to making a choice, and to supporting it thereafter, if the possibility passes the test. Team members may have quite different and incompatible tests that they view as valid, meaning that multiple tests may need to be applied for a given condition. However, in practice, groups tend to find themselves coalescing around a single acid test, especially if they take their cue from the most skeptical member of the team.

6. Conduct Tests

The test design process leads to the actual testing phase and the analysis of results. Here, we recommend taking what we sometimes call the lazy person's approach to strategy. Simply put, first test the things you're most dubious about. Take the condition the team feels is the least likely to hold up, and test it first. If the team's suspicion is right, that possibility will be eliminated without the need to test any of the other conditions. The possibility has already failed an essential test, so no more tests are necessary. If, on the other hand, the possibility passes the first test, move on to the condition with the next-lowest confidence level, and so on. Since testing is often the most expensive and time-consuming part of the choice process, this approach can save enormous amounts of resources, reducing the number of tests that must be performed in total, as possibilities fall away after just one or two tests.

This is an important feature by which the reverse-engineering process diverges profoundly from the process used in most strategy efforts. The typical process, whether internal or outsourced to consultants, features a relatively standard suite of analyses. Rather than frame the choice, understand the conditions, order the barriers, and analyze only the binding constraints—as the team does in reverse engineering—the typical approach analyzes everything in parallel. That means, in practice, a whole lot of analysis, much of which is not essential to making the decision. Furthermore, because of the wide scope of analysis, the standard process tends to accidentally sacrifice depth for breadth (i.e., analyses are a mile wide and an inch deep because the time and financial costs to do a deep analysis across the board would be prohibitive). To generate choice and commitment, companies actually need analysis that is an inch wide and a mile deep—focused precisely on the concerns that prevent the team from choosing and going deep enough in that particular area to meet the team's standard of proof. That is what reverse engineering enables you to do: probe precisely and deeply into the barriers to choice.

With Olay, for example, the price test came first. When tests showed that Olay could command a price in the $20 range, the team tested the retailer condition: would retailers partner with P&G on this initiative? Detailed conversations with a core group of P&G's most important retailers suggested that they would. Then P&G needed to convince itself that it would be able to create that holistic masstige user experience in conjunction with its key retail partners. It did so by designing, prototyping, and testing that experience.

7. Choose

In a standard process, choosing is difficult, acrimonious, and time-consuming. At an off-site meeting, participants are presented with binders full of analyses. They are asked to frame and make choices in one fell swoop on the basis of that data. With the stakes high and the logic poorly articulated, these meetings and the resultant choices rarely work out terribly well. In this reverse-engineering process, on the other hand, the choice-making step becomes simple and even anticlimactic. The team needs only to review the test results and make the choice dictated by the pattern of results. In essence, the choice makes itself; there is no need for serious debate at this late juncture. So it was with Olay; the masstige option became the clear and obvious choice.

That, in sum, is the process for choosing between possibilities for where to play and how to win. First, frame a choice. Second, explore possibilities to broaden the set of mutually exclusive possibilities. Third, for each possibility, ask, what would have to be true for this to be a great idea, using the logic flow framework to structure your thinking. Fourth, determine which of the conditions is the least likely to actually hold true. Fifth, design tests against those crucial barriers to choice. Six, conduct tests. Finally, in light of the outcome of the tests and how those outcomes stack up against predetermined standards of proof, select the best strategic choice possibility. This process broadens the possibilities up front and then systematically narrows the field. It leverages different perspectives to enrich the discussion, rather than bogging it down.

REVERSE-ENGINEERING DOS AND DON'TS

✓ Don't spend a lot of time up front analyzing everything you can; instead, use reverse engineering to pinpoint only what you really need to know.

✓ Do frame a clear and important choice up front; make it real and significant.

✓ Do explore a wide range of where-to-play and how-to-win possibilities, rather than narrowing the list early on to those that feel realistic; unexpected possibilities often have interesting and helpful elements that can otherwise be dismissed out of hand. Learn from them.

✓ Do stay focused on the most important question (what would have to be true for this to be a winning possibility?), listing the conditions under which this possibility would be a really good one.

✓ Don't forget to go back and eliminate any nice-to-have conditions; every condition should be truly binding—if it weren't true, you wouldn't pursue the possibility.

✓ Do encourage skeptics to express concerns at the specify-barriers stage; have them articulate the precise nature of their concerns about specific conditions.

✓ Don't have proponents of a given possibility set and perform the tests; ask the skeptics to do it. If the skeptics are satisfied in the end, everyone else will be too.

✓ Do test the biggest barrier first. Start with the condition the group feels is least likely to be true. If it isn't true, the conditions required do not hold and you can stop testing.

✓ Do use a facilitator to run the reverse-engineering process; it helps to have someone to attend to process and group dynamics as you work through the thinking tasks.

THE MOST IMPORTANT QUESTION IN STRATEGY

Roger L. Martin

The biggest lessons can come from the biggest mistakes. In the realm of strategy, mine sure did. The most demoralizing experience in my consulting career became my most important lesson.

In 1990, I was working with the newly appointed CEO of a regional consumer products company. The firm (unnamed here, for obvious reasons) had dominant market share in its relatively small market. During the engagement, an investment bank approached the CEO with a chance to bid for the leading competitor in a contiguous region. The target had been acquired several years earlier in a leveraged buy-out for a price of $180 million. The company was now being offered at $120 million. Intrigued, the CEO asked me to conduct an analysis of the opportunity.

My team performed a detailed analysis and came to the conclusion that the acquisition was a bad idea. The competitive dynamics of the target's regional market suggested a bleak future for the offered firm. While the target did have the leading share, its position was being rapidly eroded by a new low-cost entrant that had turned a happy duopoly into a tough three-way battle. This was an industry in which only the top two players tended to make decent returns, because of the scale economies of distribution, and the target was arguably the most vulnerable of the three players. No wonder the buy-out firm was attempting to unload it at a substantial loss. My client was tempted by the discounted price tag, but even at $120 million, this was clearly a very bad idea—and we told him so in our presentation.

The CEO acted on our analysis and told the investment bankers that he'd pass on the opportunity. So far, so good. However, about a year later, the CEO called to inform me that he could now acquire the target for a pittance—just $20 million. I begged him not to do it until I updated the analysis, and he agreed to give me the weekend. I dived back in. One more year of market share and financial information confirmed to me that the target was in a death spiral. While it had made a profit in 1990, I projected that by 1992, it would be in a loss position. I couldn't see any way that the end could be stopped or even slowed.

I came back with a deck of about a hundred slides. The cover note was succinct and to the point: "Your answer should be 'no' at any price. If you buy this, you will destroy the company and your career. Please don't do it. Please just say no."

He said yes. He bought the company at $20 million. At that price, the CEO said, a number one market share player with a strong branded position was a steal, an opportunity that simply couldn't be passed up.

He should have passed. The acquired company went almost immediately into the red. Losses accelerated. Because of prohibitive shutdown costs, the acquired business became unsalable at any price. The parent company went into a performance swoon and had to start selling off well-performing divisions to fund the losses at the acquired company. In 1994, the CEO was fired. In 1999, the once strong and independent parent company was folded into a much bigger company. Eventually, the still-horribly performing division was sold to another industry player.

Initially, I blamed the CEO for his bad judgment. The case was clear and he had ignored sound advice. I went on to other clients and continued to practice the way I had always practiced. But now I was bothered by a nagging question. Why had this intelligent and to-then successful CEO acted as he had? What led him to ignore the advice he had paid me for? I didn't have a good answer, and the question kept rolling around in my head.

Then, in 1994, I was consulting to a mining company that was facing a decision to invest in an aging mine or close it down. We held a meeting with a group of about ten executives, split evenly between those from the mine and those from the head office. There were plenty of options on the table and many opinions about the options. Suddenly, I had a flashback to the acquisition experience; in that moment, I realized that while I had a strong view as to which of the options was best, it actually didn't matter a whit what I thought. I now understood that what mattered was what the rest of the folks around the table thought; they were the ones who were going to have to take action one way or the other, not me. Unfortunately, they were all over the map. The mine managers and head-office managers were on opposite pages; head office favored the shutdown option, and mine management favored a variety of investment options.

At an impasse, an idea popped into my head. Rather than have them talk about what they thought was true about the various options, I would ask them to specify *what would have to be true* for the option on the table to be a fantastic choice. The result was magical. Clashing views turned into collaboration to really understand the logic of the options. Rather than having people attempt to convince others of the merits of options, the options themselves did the convincing (or failed to do so). In this moment, the best role of the consultant became clear to me: don't attempt to convince clients which choice is best; run a process that enables them to convince themselves.

Around the same time, I was consulting to an R&D-intensive industrial products company on its strategy. As part of my work there, company leaders asked me to help them with their advanced research portfolio. They were experiencing low success rates out of the portfolio, and problematically, projects would incur lots of expenses before being killed relatively close to the point of commercialization when it became clear that the business case didn't make sense. They asked for help in thinking about how to improve the process.

Excited about my discovery, I trotted out my new favorite question: what would have to be true? Early on in the life of a research project, we would ask, what would have to be true about each box of the logic flow diagram for this project to produce a commercial success? This marked the first time that I used the logic flow in this fashion. Again, the impact was immediate and positive. Some projects were canceled because once conditions were laid out, it was clear to the research team that the project had no hope of commercialization: all those conditions simply couldn't be true. For other projects, the order of activities changed dramatically. The "what would have to be true?" question revealed that certain issues had to be addressed right away, rather than after lots of additional spending had been done on less important questions.

From there, I used the most important question in strategy— what would have to be true?—to build an entirely new methodology for thinking through choices. It became the heart of my consulting practice and is the only strategy process I use to this day.

THE POWER OF AN OUTSIDE STRATEGY PARTNER

A.G. Lafley

CEO is an extraordinarily lonely job when done well. The CEO is the chief external officer with primary responsibility for translating the meaningful outside into winning strategies for the business and the organization. This means choosing what business or businesses to be in and which to exit, to shut down, or not to enter. This means balancing the delivery of an acceptable return from current businesses and investing in businesses that will ensure steady growth and a strong return in the future. This means setting the standards for how an organization will behave and setting the bar high for performance. In contrast to the CEO, most company employees are more inward-focused. The content of their work and the nature of their working relationships inevitably draw their attention inside the company. The CEO may well be tempted to turn his or her attention inward as well, but consciously choosing a very few external advisers and counselors can help a CEO maintain and sustain that all-important external focus.

The board of directors is one important resource on this front. P&G added annual in-depth assessments of the overall company strategy to the board agenda. An entire meeting was dedicated to strategy, with the intent of tapping into the broad and varied experiences of outside directors and drawing on their individual and collective judgment and wisdom. The board brought experience and perspective from outside the consumer packaged goods industry. It brought a mix of domain and discipline experience, along with a level of objectivity and skepticism that added real value.

P&G engaged outside strategic consultants selectively. Most of the strategic analysis and strategy creation for businesses the company knew and understood was done in-house. Nevertheless, P&G would sometimes engage outside strategy consultants to help it with a specific opportunity. McKinsey did some important strategic work with the company during P&G's due diligence on Gillette. P&G needed to maintain absolute confidentiality and wanted a partner that could confirm or deny the company's critical hypotheses and objectively assess strategic assumptions. Strategy consultants helped P&G explore industries it was considering entering. For instance, the company commissioned a broad and deep assessment of the health-care industry to help clarify where P&G might play with competitive advantage. P&G commissioned studies of certain service sectors and of franchising business models. It also commissioned studies of specific capabilities—for example, global business services, purchasing, or strategic revenue management—to ascertain how P&G's capabilities stacked up against best-in-class global competitors. Most of these strategic studies were commissioned by the businesses or functions; only a very few were commissioned by the company.

Yet, one of the most important decisions I made was to ask Roger Martin to become my strategy alter ego and partner. I wanted someone outside P&G with whom I could talk about strategy on an ongoing basis—anytime, anywhere. I wanted an outsider who understood P&G and could masterfully work the company's internal informal network to help me get important strategic things done. Importantly, I wanted someone without an agenda (at least, without an inside P&G political agenda).

I needed someone whom I could trust implicitly and who could trust me—someone I could work with informally and in complete confidence, someone with intellectual integrity to go with moral integrity, emotional intelligence to go with IQ, and the courage to tell the emperor when he was wearing no clothes.

When I became CEO, Roger and I would set aside a day at a time, a day we could get away from our calendars, e-mails, and BlackBerries, and devote ourselves to strategic issues—of his or my choosing. We kept a running list of strategic choices to be made and worked through them to resolution. Some were dispatched in a single meeting. Others were tackled several times before succumbing. Still others stayed (and some remain) open issues.

Roger and I were determined to put a robust strategic process in place throughout P&G—the process Roger had honed at Monitor and simplified and customized to suit P&G. I invited Roger to P&G's first board of directors strategy review, where he patiently walked the outside directors through the strategic methodology that he and I had worked out. We wanted the directors to understand that our integrated set of choices approach centered on where to play and how to win. From that day on, every time P&G leaders talked or wrote about company or business unit strategies, they were described in terms of winning aspirations, where-to-play and how-to-win choices, core capabilities, and management systems.

Roger had an open invitation to attend the strategy reviews and would attend several every year. He had anytime access to me (and I to him). More importantly, he built strong relationships with most of the business and functional leaders. I encouraged

P&G leaders to work on strategic issues and questions directly with Roger or with me in real time. Roger adeptly worked these informal networks to help move business leaders and their businesses ahead strategically. I would sometimes "donate" an hour or two of my time with Roger to one of the functions or the businesses. The strategic ball advanced quite a bit in one-to-one meetings between the presidents and Roger, or between the presidents and me. I met with every president every month initially (every quarter by year ten) to work on strategy, leadership, and personnel issues. The presidents and I addressed a joint agenda collaboratively.

For the presidents, one of the advantages of working through strategic issues with Roger and not with me directly was that many of them perceived Roger as less judgmental and saw the stakes of any given conversation as a bit lower. After all, he wasn't writing or signing off on their performance evaluation, deciding whether they would be promoted, or determining their compensation. But he was helping me build the strategic capability of the organization by teaching P&G's strategy methodology in internal training sessions; by coaching business leadership teams who "hired him" to assess and review their business strategy; and by assessing and evaluating the strategic thinking skills and strategic leadership effectiveness of the company's presidents and functional leaders. Together, Roger and I were continually assessing individuals as well as coaching and teaching to improve strategic capabilities. Both of us believed that strategy could be taught and learned. But both of us also believed that it required the ability to think in an integrated and disciplined way, and the courage to work on the hard choices and then make the tough calls.

Over the course of nearly ten years, Roger was my principal external strategy adviser. Clay Christensen and Mark Johnson played the external adviser role for me on innovation, Tim Brown in design, and Kevin Roberts in leadership and branding. Stuart Scheingarten, a psychologist and "coach," helped me come to grips with what worked and what didn't work with my leadership style and effectiveness. Stuart was just beginning to make some meaningful and measurable progress with his student when he died suddenly and, sadly, too young. Clayt Daley, chief financial officer, and Gil Cloyd, chief technology officer, were my primary inside strategic partners. Clayt, Gil, and I spent much more time together than I did with any outside adviser. And every strategic decision or strategic action took their advice and counsel into serious consideration. Every M&A move, Clayt and I made together—all of the acquisitions and divestitures and the near misses, those deals that got away. On Connect + Develop and P&G's overall innovation strategy, Gil was my partner every step along the way.

But I really only shared my out-of-the-box strategic musings with Roger, which was possible because of our unique personal and professional relationships. Any CEO would be fortunate to find, outside the game, an individual who understands it so well and who is willing to work tirelessly to help you take your game to the next level.

The Endless Pursuit of Winning

I t's not getting any easier to win in the real world. The new normal is, to borrow a phrase from the US military, a VUCA environment: volatile, uncertain, complex, and ambiguous. Growth is slowing, and the pace of change is increasing. As the world continues to globalize, companies face more competition for customers and consumers than ever before. Consumers are growing more demanding and more vocal, insisting upon better performance, quality, and service, all at a better price.

Even in a VUCA world, strategy can help you win. It isn't a guarantee, but it can shorten your odds considerably. A lack of strategy has a clearer and more obvious result: it will kill you. Maybe not right away, but eventually companies without winning strategies die. A great invention or product idea can create a company, build value, and win in the marketplace for a while. But to last, the company behind that idea must answer the five strategic questions that create and sustain lasting competitive advantage.

For your own company, ask (and honestly answer):

1. Have you defined winning, and are you crystal clear about your winning aspiration?

2. Have you decided where you can play to win (and just as decisively where you will *not* play)?

3. Have you determined how, specifically, you will win where you choose to play?

4. Have you pinpointed and built your core capabilities in such a way that they enable your where-to-play and how-to-win choices?

5. Do your management systems and key measures support your other four strategic choices?

The tools and frameworks in this book are designed to help you answer these five questions and to explore the possibilities for your organization. Again, for your organization, have you used the tools to help you think through your potential choices?

- Have you used the strategy logic flow framework to understand the industry, channel, and customer values, your own relative capability and cost positions, and competitive reactions in a way that can underpin sustainable where-to-play and how-to-win choices?

- Have you reverse engineered the strategic possibilities and asked what would have to be true to ensure that this possibility is the one that gives you the best chance to win?

The strategic choice cascade, the strategic logic flow, and the reverse-engineering process represent a strategic playbook for your organization. Rather than a simple, one-way path, the plays

FIGURE C-1

The playbook

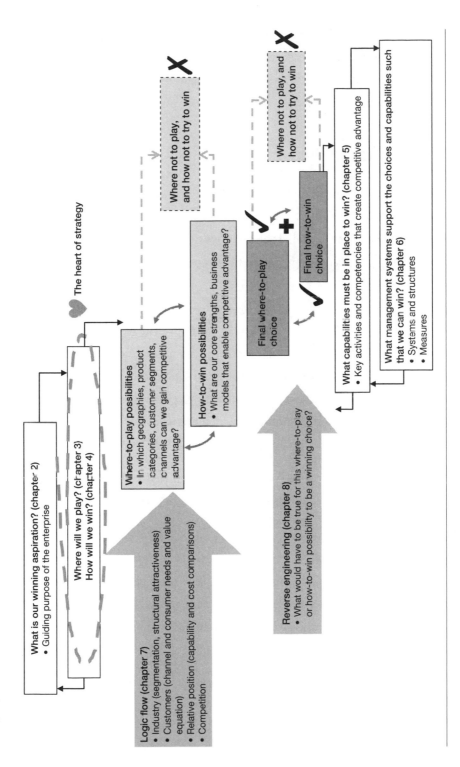

can be complex and winding; you will need to circle back, revisit, and revise. But taken together (see figure C-1), the playbook can guide your strategic thinking and help create true and lasting competitive advantage.

Six Strategy Traps

There is no perfect strategy—no algorithm that can guarantee sustainable competitive advantage in a given industry or business. But there are signals that a company has a particularly worrisome strategy. Here are six of the most common strategy traps:

1. *The do-it-all strategy:* failing to make choices, and making everything a priority. Remember, strategy is choice.

2. *The Don Quixote strategy:* attacking competitive "walled cities" or taking on the strongest competitor first, head-to-head. Remember, where to play is your choice. Pick somewhere you can have a chance to win.

3. *The Waterloo strategy:* starting wars on multiple fronts with multiple competitors at the same time. No company can do everything well. If you try to do so, you will do everything weakly.

4. *The something-for-everyone strategy:* attempting to capture all consumer or channel or geographic or category segments at once. Remember, to create real value, you have to choose to serve some constituents really well and not worry about the others.

5. *The dreams-that-never-come-true strategy:* developing high-level aspirations and mission statements that never get translated into concrete where-to-play and how-to-win choices,

core capabilities, and management systems. Remember that aspirations are not strategy. Strategy is the answer to all five questions in the choice cascade.

6. *The program-of-the-month strategy:* settling for generic industry strategies, in which all competitors are chasing the same customers, geographies, and segments in the same way. The choice cascade and activity system that supports these choices should be distinctive. The more your choices look like those of your competitors, the less likely you will ever win.

These are strategic traps to be aware of as you craft a strategy for your organization. But there are also signs that you have found a winning and defensible strategy. Let's look at these next.

Six Telltale Signs of a Winning Strategy

Because the world is so complex, it is hard to tell definitely which results are due to the strategy, which to macro factors, and which to luck. But, there are some common signs that a winning strategy is in place. Look for these, for your own business and among your competitors.

1. An activity system that looks different from any competitor's system. It means you are attempting to deliver value in a distinctive way.

2. Customers who absolutely adore you, and noncustomers who can't see why anybody would buy from you. This means you have been choiceful.

3. Competitors who make a good profit doing what they are doing. It means your strategy has left where-to-play and

how-to-win choices for competitors, who don't need to attack the heart of your market to survive.

4. More resources to spend on an ongoing basis than competitors have. This means you are winning the value equation and have the biggest margin between price and costs and the best capacity to add spending to take advantage of an opportunity or defend your turf.

5. Competitors who attack one another, not you. It means that you look like the hardest target in the (broadly defined) industry to attack.

6. Customers who look first to you for innovations, new products, and service enhancement to make their lives better. This means that your customers believe that you are uniquely positioned to create value for them.

Even companies with these telltale signs shouldn't rest, because no strategy lasts forever. All companies need to evolve their strategies—to improve, sharpen, and change to stay competitive and, ultimately, to win year after year. Ideally, companies should see strategy as a process rather than a result—adapting existing choices before business and financial results (which are always lagging indicators) start to turn down.

All strategy entails risk. But operating in a slow-growing, fast-changing, intensely competitive world without a strategy to guide you is far riskier. Leaders lead, and a good place to start leading is in strategy development for your business. Use the strategic choice cascade, the strategy logic flow, and reverse engineering of strategic choices to craft a winning strategy and sustainable competitive advantage for your organization. Play to win.

Acknowledgments

We are deeply indebted to many fine friends, colleagues, and mentors for their work, which was instrumental to this book.

First and foremost is Jennifer Riel, who served us in numerous important capacities. She was our editor in chief, but in addition to that she managed our research and conducted the P&G executive interviews, many on her own. She also cowrote and rewrote many sections of the book. We couldn't have produced this book without her brilliance, diligence, and colleagueship.

This book wouldn't have been nearly as rich without the perspectives of numerous P&G executives, including former Chairman and CEO John Pepper and current Chairman and CEO Bob McDonald. Other P&G executives, past and present, who contributed in this way are Chip Bergh, Gil Cloyd, Clayt Daley, Gina Drosos, Melanie Healey, Deb Henretta, Michael Kuremsky, Joan Lewis, Joe Listro, Jorge Mesquita, Jon Moeller, Filippo Passerini, Charlie Pierce, David Taylor, Jeff Weedman, and Craig Wynett. Also, George Roeth and Larry Peiros at Clorox were generous in providing interviews related to the Clorox/P&G joint venture on Glad products. Thank you to them and to the thousands of P&G employees whose work inspired the stories in this book.

Fiona Houslip, Claudia Kotchka, Joe Rotman, Dave Samuel, and Tomer Strolight read the penultimate draft of the book, and all provided extremely valuable comments that changed the final manuscript for the better.

Darren Karn and Patrick Blair provided us with lots of great research support.

The team at Harvard Business Review Press has been terrific as always. Our thanks to Erin Brown, Julie Devoll, Adi Ignatius, Jeff Kehoe, Allison Peter, and Erica Truxler. Superagent Tina Bennett (then of Janklow & Nesbit) did a wonderful job, as always, and we have been ably supported by Mark Fortier of Fortier Public Relations.

We also owe a huge debt of gratitude to three intellectual giants who shaped our thinking on management and strategy. First is our dear departed friend Peter Drucker, who not only shaped management thinking over three-quarters of a century, but helped both of us personally and did so in the most generous and caring way. Second is our friend and colleague Michael Porter. Many of the approaches in this book build off his seminal work in strategy. P&G's decision to engage with Michael on strategy in the mid-1980s was critical to both P&G's strategic development and our personal journeys in understanding strategy. Third is the great organizational learning scholar Chris Argyris, who taught us the importance of balancing advocacy with inquiry in communication, a concept that shaped not only our personal practices but the evolution of strategy development at P&G.

In addition, each of us would like to thank individuals within our personal circles.

Roger

My time at Monitor was seminal to the development of many of the ideas that contributed to this book. During my thirteen years there, Mark Fuller was my CEO, and he gave me great latitude and encouragement to innovate. I wouldn't have become the strategist I am today without his support and forbearance. Then there are two consultants, both of whom I hired as youngsters, who became wonderful colleagues and taught me a great deal. Sandra Pocharski worked with me on numerous projects and was a terrific thinking partner on the development of several of the most important tools in this book. Jonathan Goodman worked with me on more projects than I can count and helped me refine the consulting tools that are described in these pages. Happily, both have gone on to become among the finest senior strategy consultants in the world. They remain close friends with whom I am lucky enough to occasionally collaborate.

At the Rotman School, I am supported by a dedicated team who make it possible for me to spend some of my time writing books like this one. In addition to the aforementioned Jennifer Riel, the core team includes Vice Deans Peter Pauly and Jim Fisher, Chief Operating Officer Mary-Ellen Yeomans, Chief of Staff Suzanne Spragge, and Executive Assistant Kathryn Davis. I am so lucky to have them as colleagues.

A.G.

Thirty-three years at P&G afforded me ample opportunity to learn about business strategy and practice business leadership and management by doing. There, with clear accountability for strategy, operations, and results, I learned from my mistakes, lived with my failures, and appreciated on a daily basis my colleagues' contributions to whatever success we were able to achieve together.

I cut my teeth on strategy in what was then called the U.S. Packaged Soap and Detergent Division at P&G, one of the company's biggest, oldest, and most profitable businesses. At one time or another in my first eleven years at the company, I worked on every category and brand in the division. Working in a mature, slow-growing, highly competitive industry, I learned how to differentiate and distinguish a business, how to create competitive advantage, and how to generate meaningful value—because if we didn't, we'd go out of business. Steve Donovan, a P&G-er I worked for and with during fifteen years of my career, set the standard high for strategy, for execution, and for value creation. And he always focused on playing to win.

I was fortunate to be a part of the first Applied Strategic Management training at P&G in the late 1980s—to learn from Michael Porter and to work with Mark Fuller and Roger Martin.

It was a privilege to work with Peter Drucker from 2000 until his death in 2005 and to collaborate with him on the unique work of the CEO, which, of course, starts with strategy.

In the time I served as Chairman and CEO, P&G tried to build a network of strategic partnerships with customers, suppliers, other business partners, and even competitors (in noncompetitive industries). As P&G expanded across geographies and industries, we tried to encourage an ongoing strategic dialogue in all of the different businesses. In the course of the decade, I learned so much from my colleagues—particularly from:

- Gil Cloyd, former P&G Chief Innovation Officer, who shared my belief that P&G could and should change its strategy toward innovation;

- Clayt Daley, former P&G Chief Financial Officer, who helped me sort through industries and businesses for structural and strategic attractiveness, and P&G businesses for competitive edge; and

- P&G business and functional presidents and P&G category, country, and customer general managers (too numerous to name individually) who dialogued, discussed, and debated their where-to-play and how-to-win choices. I'm sure I drove more than a few of them crazy, pushing them to make the clearer and often harder choices required to win.

Neither *Playing to Win* nor my previous book *The Game Changer* would have happened without the caring commitment and counsel of my wife, Diana. She is my best coach and my clearest and most constructive critic. She encourages me to translate my personal experiences and learning into simple concepts and insights that logically lead to practical actions for others to follow. That is what Roger and I have sought to do in this book.

P&G's Performance

The stories in this book are taken from the years 2000 to 2009. Over those years, P&G sales doubled and profits quadrupled. Earnings per share increased 12 percent per year. P&G's share price increased by more than 80 percent in a decade that saw the S&P 500 go down overall. Company market capitalization more than doubled, placing P&G among the most valuable companies in the world. The company was able to deliver significantly more value, create competitive advantage, and perform at a consistently high level over the decade.

While these facts capture something about the performance of the company over the decade, they do not directly answer these questions: did the strategic choices deliver winning results? And if so, which specific choices delivered which business and financial results? These answers are captured in tables A-1 and A-2, which illustrate the specific business and financial contributions of the where-to-play and how-to-win choices made in the period.

TABLE A-1

Results of P&G's where-to-play choices, 2000 and 2009

Where-to-play choice	Parameter	Results 2000	2009
Grow from the core	Core categories, percentage of P&G sales	55	79
	Core categories, percentage of P&G profits	59	83
	Number of brands with $1 billion (or more) annual sales	10	25
	Billion-dollar brands, percentage of sales	54	69
	Core categories, sales compound annual growth rate (CAGR)	11%	
Extend into beauty	Beauty, sales CAGR	15%	
	Beauty, percentage of P&G sales	16	33
	Beauty, percentage of P&G sales growth	44	
	Beauty, percentage of P&G profit growth	42	
Expand into emerging markets	Emerging markets, sales CAGR	13%	
	Emerging markets, percentage of P&G sales	20	32
	Emerging markets, percentage of P&G sales growth	42	
	Emerging markets, percentage of P&G profit growth	29	

TABLE A-2

Results of P&G's how-to-win choices, 2000 and 2009

Other key performance measures	*2000*	*2009*
Gross margin	46%	52%
Free cash flow	$3.5 billion	$15 billion
Capital expenditures (percentage of sales)	7.6	4.3
Global business services (percentage of sales)	6.5	3.1
R&D (percentage of sales)	4.8	2.5
Marketing (percentage of sales)	14	15

The strategies that were developed between 2000 and 2009 generated significant value for the company and shareholders. Yet no strategy is perfect, and P&G during this decade had its share of disappointments and failures:

- *Coffee.* While P&G's Folgers won the battle against Maxwell House for packaged coffee leadership in grocery and mass channels, Starbucks, Nespresso, and Keurig all won in the bigger game, creating strategies that captured more coffee consumption and significant value creation. Folgers bid and lost three times for the Starbucks packaged-coffee contract. It tested and failed in a partnership to create its own pod-plus-machine coffee system. P&G lost the larger war. In 2008, the company sold the profitable $1.7 billion Folgers business to Smuckers.

- *Pringles.* P&G wasn't able to realize the full potential of its $1.5 billion Pringles snacks business and sold it to Kellogg in 2011.

- *Pharmaceuticals.* P&G could not obtain regulatory approval for its Intrinsa testosterone patch for women; nor could the company form partnerships for, or swap out, its prescription pharmaceutical business for over-the-counter brands to create more value. P&G sold its $2.5 billion pharmaceuticals business in 2009.

- *M&A.* P&G missed on a number of merger and acquisition opportunities. It was unable to close a joint venture with Coca-Cola in the juice beverages and snacks business—a venture that would have created significant value. Nor could P&G close an acquisition for a major, global skin-care brand, although it did acquire DDF (Doctor's Dermatological Formula), a small US niche brand.

- *New brands.* P&G was unable to create successful new brands with Dryel, Fit, Olay Cosmetics, Physique, Tempo, or Torengos.

Despite the disappointments and failures, P&G made sufficiently good strategic choices to create enough sustainable competitive advantage and to deliver enough consistent value creation to put the company among the leading performers in its industry, on the Dow Jones 30 and the *Fortune* 50. So, it can be tempting to assume that P&G's strategies in the first decade of the twenty-first century are the right strategies for the company (or category, or brand) moving forward.

But no strategy lasts forever. Strategies need continual improvement and updating. Competitors have copied P&G's strategies—on innovation, on branding, and the like—to an extent that renders P&G's resultant strategy less distinctive and decisive. The consumer packaged goods industry is expanding into emerging markets in a shared search for growth, making this approach a more common strategy across the industry and less powerful for individual players. Approaches that were significant sources of competitive advantage must be revisited and revised as contexts change. This is the challenge that faces the next generation of P&G leaders, just as it challenged leaders in 2000 and will challenge succeeding generations. Every P&G leader has needed to change the strategy they inherited in light of the changing context, and P&G's current and future leaders will have to do the same.

Historically P&G has risen to meet its challenges over a 175-year-plus history. This legacy of strategic and careful decision-making should serve P&G well if the management team keeps searching for unique where-to-play and how-to-win choices that set the company apart. Winning through distinctive choices is the always-and-forever job of every strategist.

The Microeconomic Foundations of Strategy and the Two Ways to Win

I t may seem hard to believe that there are only two possible ways to win—low cost or differentiation. Why only those two, people often wonder, and what drives this dynamic?

This outcome is driven by the fundamental microeconomic foundations of strategy. A firm can face only two fundamental economic conditions, one of which gives rise to low-cost strategies, and another that gives rise to differentiation strategies. In microeconomics, the two central structures are demand and supply, and where they cross, the price is determined.

Structure of Demand

Demand is a measure of consumer willingness to purchase a given product or service. Each individual buyer has his or her own demand curve: if the price is high, the person will buy less; if it is low, he or she will buy more. The utility of the product to each individual

FIGURE B-1

Construction of industry demand curve

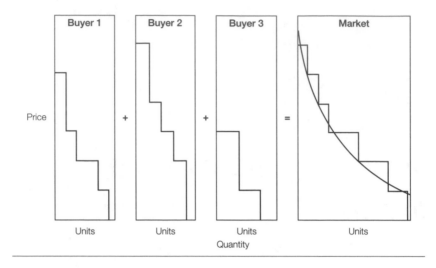

will determine how much is purchased at what price, and not every consumer has the same utility for a given product or service. A hungry person has a higher utility for a turkey sandwich than does a satiated person. So, each individual buyer has his or her own demand curve. Nevertheless, you can calculate the industry demand by aggregating the individual demand curves together. The industry curve follows the same basic principles as individual demand curves—the curve slopes downward as higher prices produce lower demand and lower prices produce higher demand (figure B-1).

Structure of Supply

A similar dynamic occurs on the supply side. Each firm is willing to produce a certain amount of output, given the prevailing price level. That supply has costs associated with it, and the most crucial type of cost for our purposes is the variable cost of producing

FIGURE B-2

Construction of industry supply curve

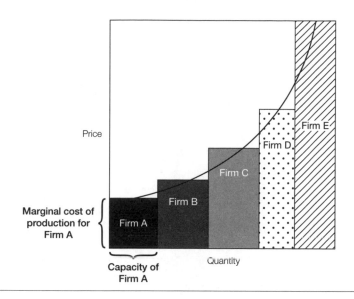

another unit of output. Some costs don't vary with the production of another unit—such as R&D or advertising—while other costs increase when an additional unit is produced—such as raw materials or direct labor. These latter costs are most important in driving price.

Firms can be arrayed on an industry supply curve on the basis of their variable cost of production, using the marginal cost to produce an additional item, from low to high (figure B-2). By their very nature, supply curves are upward sloping; the lower the price in the market, the less quantity will be produced.

Where the supply crosses the downward-sloping demand curve, price and quantity are set by the proverbial invisible hand (figure B-3). This is the case for all kinds of products and services. However, the dynamics work differently in a commodity versus a distinct or unique offering.

FIGURE B-3

The intersection of supply and demand

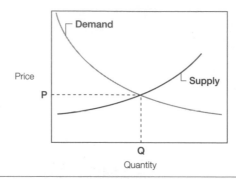

Competition in Commodity Products and Services

In a classic commodity industry, such as gold, there are multiple producers. Buyers see the offerings from these different producers as essentially identical—an ounce of gold is pretty much like any other ounce of gold. In such a market, a producer has no choice but to accept the market price. If it prices even a little bit above the prevailing market price, buyers will go en masse to competitors and the producer will sell nothing. If the producer prices below the prevailing market price, it will just be throwing away some of its possible profit margin.

Thus, while the industry demand curve is actually downward sloping—higher gold price will generate lower demand and lower gold price will generate higher demand—individual producers in the commodity market feel as if they are facing a flat demand curve. There is no opportunity to price higher or lower to reduce or increase demand. The price is the price. It may well fluctuate over time, but not due to anything an individual producer does.

In such a market, relative cost position is the sole determinant of competitiveness and profitability. Price is established at the point at which the aggregate industry demand curve intersects with

FIGURE B-4

Cost position determines competitiveness

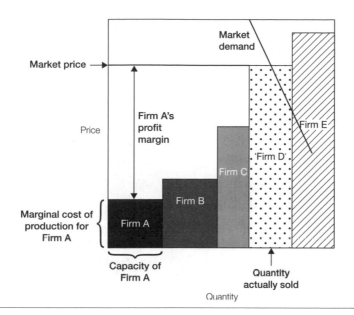

the aggregate industry supply curve, and the latter is created by the variable cost of the marginal producer. Once that price is established, each firm earns a profit margin over and above its variable costs, the size of which is determined by its relative cost position (figure B-4).

In the industry in figure B-4, firms survive in this market as long as the market price exceeds their marginal cost of production. So, firms A, B, C, and D remain in the market, but firm E must reduce its cost or exit. The most efficient firm, firm A, earns healthy profits despite the intense competition. The same dynamics of price-setting and profitability are at work in all commodity industries. Pricing is bid down until the marginal player just covers its variable costs. If buyers were to attempt to bid down prices further, firm D would go out of business and there would be an undersupply, which would drive prices back up.

FIGURE B-5

Pulp and paper

Example cost curve: North American uncoated free sheet (standard photocopier paper)

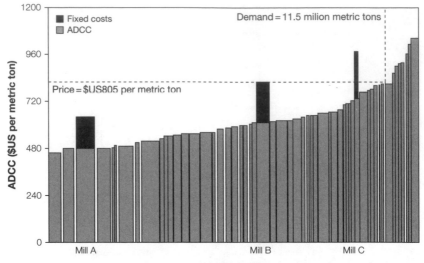

The bars represent the various companies that make free sheet.

The tricky thing is that firms have to pay for all of their fixed costs plus their return on investment out of the margin between their variable costs and the market price. Figure B-5 illustrates the impact of fixed cost on net profitability in the uncoated free sheet (i.e., standard photocopier paper). The data is from an analysis in the mid-1990s, but the principles remain unchanged.

In this industry, low-cost mill A has variable costs of about $480 per metric ton. Market price is $805 per metric ton, providing a margin of $325 per metric ton. Out of that, the mill has fixed costs to cover, which work out to about $150 per ton across its total volume. That leaves a profit of $175 per ton for mill A.

Mill B also has variable costs that leave a substantial margin between costs and price, but in its case, its fixed costs (which are spread across lower output, as indicated by the width of the bar) take up the entire margin; mill B barely breaks even at the end of the year. However, since the mill would have those fixed costs at least for the medium term even if it stopped producing, it is better for mill B to continue to produce paper, earning a margin that goes toward paying those fixed costs. The owners of mill B rail against the irrational dynamics of the industry, arguing that the industry has pricing levels too low for a producer to make a decent return on capital. Unfortunately for mill B, it is quite possible to make a good profit in the business, but only if you are in the bottom portion of the variable-cost curve.

In a still worse position is tiny mill C. Its variable costs are high but below the price level. Unfortunately, its fixed costs per ton are so high that at the end of the year, it shows a substantial loss. Mill C stays in business, hoping that demand rises and shifts the demand curve out to cross the supply curve at the right side of the chart, which would push mill C into a profit (and mill A into obscene profits).

Sadly, demand rarely rises in the way that mill C hopes. Instead, what typically happens is that new entrants look at competitors like mill A, see the money to be made in the industry, and then figure out a way to enter with even lower costs than those incurred by mill A. These new entrants analyze everything mill A does and then do it a bit better, investing higher levels of capital to produce a low-cost position. The entry of a new low-cost firm (firm Z in figure B-6) pushes the entire supply curve to the right, causing the demand curve to cross the supply curve at a lower price and the price to fall for all players.

Whereas firm D used to be breakeven on variable costs, it is now substantially in the hole before fixed costs. Firm C is now breakeven on a variable-cost basis. In the US scheduled air travel market, firm Z is Southwest Airlines, whose entry and growth has made it increasingly rough for all the traditional carriers, which argue that the market is irrational. Actually, the market is utterly rational.

Evolution of commodity markets

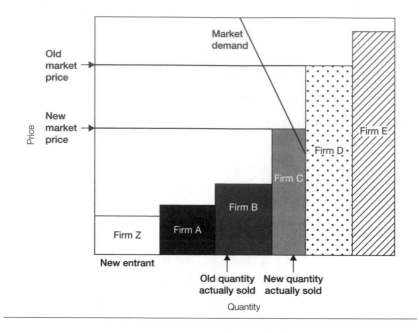

This is what happens to commodities across the world. A new low-cost entry drives down the prices—whether by way of fast-growing Southern Hemisphere eucalyptus in pulp and paper or cheap Peruvian mines in nickel. Though some commentators argue that commodity prices are rising, these prices have fallen consistently over the past two hundred years on a real-price basis. Figure B-7 shows the real price of a basket of commodities (sized based on the world consumption proportions of these commodities) from 1801 to 1999. While there have been dramatic upticks, the long-term trend is unmistakably downward.

This doesn't mean that competing in a commodity business is bad. It just means that if you do, you need to be at the bottom of the variable-cost curve or you won't have much fun!

FIGURE B-7

Falling commodity prices

Commodity price index in real US dollars, 1801–1999.

Source: BMO Capital Markets Economic Research.
Index of 180 = 100.

Competition in a Unique Product or Service

When a firm offers a product or service that buyers consider unique, the pricing and profit dynamics are quite different. The firm providing the unique offering is a price-setter, not a price-taker; the demand for the unique offering depends upon the price the firm sets—the higher the price, the lower the demand and vice versa. But this time, because the producer of a unique offering serves the entire market, the firm feels the shift in demand directly. Unlike in a commodity business, here price setting is one of the producer's most important choices.

In a differentiated offering, there is an optimal price: the price at which the marginal revenue is equal to the marginal cost to the producer. The marginal-revenue curve falls faster than the demand curve because the firm needs to drop the price to all customers, not just the marginal customer, when pursuing incremental demand.

FIGURE B-8

Maximizing profit from a unique product

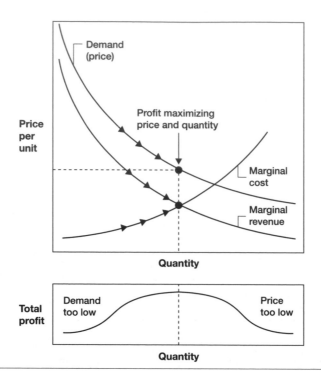

As a consequence, marginal revenue doesn't increase by the price of the incremental unit. It increases by that amount less the revenue lost on each prior unit. At some point, the marginal revenue is lower than the marginal cost and the firm has pushed price too far, as shown in figure B-8.

The Two Fundamental Ways to Win

The foregoing gives rise to the two fundamental ways to win. A firm can choose to offer a similar offering or a unique offering, and each offering has one and only one form of strategy associated with it.

In the case of a similar offering, a firm does not attempt to convince the customer that its offering is unique. The offering may not be a pure commodity like an ounce of gold, but it might be a sixty-watt light bulb or a sheet of drywall or even a standard "Wintel" PC. The distinction is that the firm does not attempt to position its offering as sufficiently unique to warrant a price premium of any sort. Once that decision has been made, the only strategy to follow for competitive advantage is a low-cost one—that is, a strategy of being in the bottom quarter to third of the cost curve. If a firm is a price-taker, that is the only way to achieve a sustainable competitive advantage. It needs to focus its primary energies on defending its place in the lower third of the industry cost curve, even against new entrants that may come to the market with new techniques or technologies. Note that while being in the lower third of the cost curve tends to ensure strong profitability at least in the short to medium term, a firm is vulnerable to the potential actions of the very lowest-cost player. There is only one truly lowest-cost player, and if that player wishes to grow faster or punish other competitors higher up on the cost curve, it can start a price war that drives prices down for all competitors. And because it has the very lowest-cost position, the firm can weather the price war better than all other competitors.

In the case of a unique offering, the firm needs to differentiate in a way that the customer values sufficiently to pay a price premium, enabling the firm to earn an attractive return. This is a differentiation strategy. In essence, for a particular group of customers, the firm is a monopoly supplier. The customers don't think that they have a choice of an identical offering; they would have to switch to a different sort of offering if they choose not to buy from this firm. In a differentiation strategy, the firm needs to focus its energies on maintaining its uniqueness in the eyes of the customers. Only if its offerings seem unique to the customers will a firm continue to earn a price premium over nonunique competitors and hence maintain its competitive advantage.

Regardless of the industry, firms can play as the low-cost competitor. Even if the product in an industry is a commodity (e.g., uncoated free sheet), the offering of a firm in that industry need not be undifferentiated. The firm could differentiate its offering by providing better customer service, more consistent delivery, better integration with the downstream buyer's operations, and so on. And even in industries dominated by branded, differentiated players, there can be nonunique players that win through a low-cost strategy. Certainly the store-controlled brands in the food and consumer packaged goods businesses are excellent examples of this approach.

So firms can always choose to win as either a cost leader or a differentiator. What they can't do is win any other way. Due to the fundamental microeconomics of business, there are only two ways to win: higher margin through lower cost or higher margin through differentiation.

Notes

Introduction

1. Michael Porter, *Competitive Strategy: Techniques for Analyzing Industries and Competitors* (New York: Simon & Schuster, 1980).

2. In 2007, I (R. M.) wrote a book about integrative thinking (Roger Martin, *The Opposable Mind: How Successful Leaders Win Through Integrative Thinking* [Boston: Harvard Business School Press]). In the book, I argue that when highly successful leaders are faced with a difficult choice between opposing models, neither of which is particularly attractive, rather than choose, the leaders generally build a new model that is superior to both models but contains elements of each. Because I also write frequently about strategy as choice, as we do in this book, some readers have suggested that I am internally inconsistent: successful leaders either don't choose (per *The Opposable Mind*) or do choose (per *Playing to Win*). I would offer a different perspective. All the integrative thinkers that I chronicled in *The Opposable Mind*, from Bob Young of Red Hat to Isadore Sharp of Four Seasons Hotels and Resorts to Victoria Hale of the Institute for One World Health to A.G. Lafley, made many key choices. In fact, all made clear and distinctive choices about where to play and how to win. The difference between these leaders and their competitors is not in the act of choosing, but rather in the standards they apply to the choice. Integrative thinkers set a high bar for where to play and how to win. They assess existing options or business models against that high bar, and when no existing model offers a reasonable probability of winning, integrative thinkers refuse resolutely to choose between those existing alternatives. In my view, there is no inconsistency between integrative thinking and strategy choice making. Integrative thinkers set a high bar to make strategy choices that really pay off for their organizations.

Chapter One

1. To keep things as simple as possible, we have tried to consistently use the same terminology throughout the book. Because these terms may not be universally defined in the same way, we will specify what we mean in a few cases. For our purposes, *consumers* are end users—the people who buy P&G's products and take them home for themselves and their families. *Customers*, on the other hand, are retailers—the stores that serve as channels or middlemen between P&G and consumers. P&G sells to customers, who sell to consumers.

2. All quotes from Michael Kuremsky are from a telephone interview with our colleague, Jennifer Riel, November 24, 2010.

3. Unless otherwise noted, all brands are registered trademarks of Procter & Gamble.

4. All quotes from Gina Drosos are from a telephone interview with Jennifer Riel, November 1, 2010.

5. All quotes from Joe Listro are from a telephone interview with Jennifer Riel, November 12, 2010.

6. All quotes from Chip Bergh are from a telephone interview with Jennifer Riel, November 1, 2010.

Chapter Two

1. James Mateja, "Why Saturn Is So Important to GM," *Chicago Tribune*, January 13, 1985, 1.

2. Bill Vlasic and Nick Bunkley, "Detroit's Mr. Fix-It Takes on Saturn," *New York Times*, September 20, 2009, BU-1.

3. Ben Klayman, "GM Focusing on Profits, Not U.S. Market Share: CEO," Reuters, January 9, 2012, www.reuters.com/article/2012/01/10/us-gm-usshare-idUSTRE8081MU20120110.

4. Vlasic and Bunkley, "Detroit's Mr. Fix-It Takes on Saturn."

5. All quotes from Filippo Passerini are from an interview with Roger Martin and Jennifer Riel, Cincinnati, November 18, 2010.

Chapter Three

1. All quotes from Charlie Pierce are from an interview with Roger Martin and Jennifer Riel, Cincinnati, November 18, 2010.

2. Bob McDonald, speech delivered to Global Business Leadership Council Year End Meeting, November 11, 2009, P&G Global Employee webcast.

3. "Tesco Loses More Market Share," *Guardian* (Manchester), April 24, 2012, www.guardian.co.uk/business/2012/apr/24/tesco-loses-market-share-kantar-worldpanel.

4. "Global 2000: Top Retail Companies; Wal-Mart," *Forbes*, accessed July 12, 2012, www.forbes.com/pictures/eggh45lgg/wal-mart-stores-3/#gallerycontent.

5. Chip Bergh, telephone interview with Jennifer Riel, November 1, 2010.

6. Ben Steverman, "Twenty Products That Rocked the Stock Market: Hits or Misses," *Bloomberg Businessweek*, January 2010, http://imA.G.es.businessweek.com/ss/10/01/0127_20_stock_market_rocking_products/17.htm.

Chapter Four

1. ForceFlex and Kitchen Catcher are registered trademarks of The Clorox Company.

2. All quotes from Jeff Weedman are from an interview with Jennifer Riel, Cincinnati, January 5, 2012.

3. All quotes from Larry Peiros are from a telephone interview with Jennifer Riel, March 6, 2012.

4. All quotes from Joan Lewis are from a telephone interview with Jennifer Riel on January 19, 2012.

5. All quotes from Deb Henretta are from a telephone interview with Jennifer Riel, November 2, 2010.

Chapter Five

1. The combined value of the merger was $342 billion at closing, and AOL shareholders got 55 percent of the company. The spinoff was for one-twelfth of the prevailing price, which was $38 billion.

2. Andrew Davidson, "The Razor-Sharp P&G Boss," *Sunday Times* (London), December 3, 2006, 6.

3. All quotes from Clayt Daley are from a telephone interview with Roger Martin and Jennifer Riel, December 22, 2010.

4. All quotes from Chip Bergh are from a telephone interview with Jennifer Riel, November 1, 2010.

5. Damon Jones, "Latest Innovations: Gillette Guard," Gillette fact sheet, accessed July 16, 2012, www.pg.com/en_US/downloads/innovation/factsheet_final_Gillette_Guard.pdf.

6. Ellen Bryon, "Gillette's Latest Innovation in Razors: The 11-Cent Blade," *Wall Street Journal*, October 1, 2010, http://online.wsj.com/article/SB10001424052748704789404575524273890970954.html.

7. P&G eStore, Gillette page, accessed July 16, 2012, www.pgestore.com/Gillette/gillette-mega,default,sc.html.

8. All quotes from Filippo Passerini are from an interview with Roger Martin and Jennifer Riel, Cincinnati, November 18, 2010.

9. Michael Porter, "What Is Strategy?" *Harvard Business Review*, November–December 1996, 61–78.

10. Ibid.

11. Porter uses activity systems to capture the strategy of a business unit. In his conception, the largest nodes are the key strategic themes—the elements of the strategy that set the firm apart and create competitive advantage. The links between them represent important reinforcing relationships. The subordinate nodes in the map are the supporting activities, the tightly linked systems that support and enhance the functioning of the core themes. In our adaptation of Porter's activity systems, we consider the largest hubs the core capabilities rather than strategic themes, the themes having already been captured in the answers to where to play and how to win.

Chapter Six

1. All quotes from David Taylor are from an interview with Roger Martin and Jennifer Riel, Cincinnati, November 18, 2010.

2. All quotes from Melanie Healey are from a telephone interview with Jennifer Riel, November 15, 2010.

3. Anonymous, interview with Jennifer Riel, November 2010.

4. A.G. had read and been influenced by Jan Carlzon, *Moments of Truth* (Cambridge, MA: Ballinger, 1987). In it, Carlzon, former CEO of Scandinavian Airline System, recounts how he turned a dowdy state airline around through a customer-first orientation. Though the application of "moments of truth" to the consumer context wasn't entirely new,

Carlzon powerfully articulated how an understanding of those moments helped transform his company.

5. All quotes from Jon Moeller are from an interview with Roger Martin and Jennifer Riel, Cincinnati, November 18, 2010.

6. All quotes from Deb Henretta are from a telephone interview with Jennifer Riel, November 2, 2010.

7. NPI is a measure of customer loyalty that tracks the degree to which consumers are not just users but advocates of a brand, specifically asking whether a consumer would be likely to recommend a brand or product to others. For more on Net Promoter Score, see Fred Reichheld, *The Ultimate Question: Driving Good Profits and True Growth* (Boston: Harvard Business School Publishing, 2006).

Index

About the Authors

A.G. LAFLEY is the former Chairman of the Board, President, and Chief Executive Officer of Procter & Gamble. Under Lafley's leadership, P&G sales doubled, profits quadrupled, P&G's market value increased by more than $100 billion, and its portfolio of billion-dollar brands—such as Tide, Pampers, Olay, and Gillette—grew from ten to twenty-four as a result of his focus on winning strategic choices, consumer-driven innovation, and reliable, sustainable growth.

Lafley has been awarded some of the highest honors in business, including *Chief Executive* magazine's CEO of the Year, the Peter G. Peterson Award for Business Statesmanship, the Edison Achievement Award for innovation, and the Warren Bennis Award for Excellence in Leadership. He has also been inducted into the Advertising Hall of Fame and *Industry Week* Manufacturing Hall of Fame.

Today, Lafley consults on business and innovation strategy, advises on CEO succession and executive leadership development, and coaches experienced, new, and aspiring CEOs.

ROGER L. MARTIN is Dean of the Rotman School of Management at the University of Toronto and an adviser to CEOs on strategy, design, innovation, and integrative thinking. Martin has written widely on these subjects and has published seven books: *Fixing the Game*; *The Design of Business*; *The Opposable Mind*; *The Responsibility Virus*; *Canada: What It Is, What It Can Be* (with James Milway); *Diaminds* (with Mihnea Moldoveanu); and *The Future of the MBA* (also with Moldoveanu).

In 2011 Martin placed sixth on the Thinkers50 list, a biannual ranking of the world's most influential business thinkers. In 2010 he was named one of the twenty-seven most influential designers in the world by *BusinessWeek*. In 2007 *BusinessWeek* named him a B-School All-Star—one of the ten most influential business professors in the world.

A Canadian from Wallenstein, Ontario, Martin holds an AB in economics from Harvard College and an MBA from Harvard Business School.